THE ENCYCLOPEDIA OF PSYCHOACTIVE DRUGS

IN 25 VOLUMES
Each title on a specific drug or drug-related problem

ALCOHOL
Alcohol *and Alcoholism*
Alcohol *Customs and Rituals*
Alcohol *Teenage Drinking*

HALLUCINOGENS
Flowering Plants *Magic in Bloom*
LSD *Visions or Nightmares*
Marijuana *Its Effects on Mind & Body*
Mushrooms *Psychedelic Fungi*
PCP *The Dangerous Angel*

NARCOTICS
Heroin *The Street Narcotic*
Methadone *Treatment for Addiction*
Prescription Narcotics *The Addictive Painkillers*

NON-PRESCRIPTION DRUGS
Over-the-Counter Drugs *Harmless or Hazardous?*

SEDATIVE HYPNOTICS
Barbiturates *Sleeping Potion or Intoxicant*
Inhalants *The Toxic Fumes*
Methaqualone *The Quest for Oblivion*
Tranquillizers *The Cost of Calmness*

STIMULANTS
Amphetamines *Danger in the Fast Lane*
Caffeine *The Most Popular Stimulant*
Cocaine *A New Epidemic*
Nicotine *An Old-Fashioned Addiction*

UNDERSTANDING DRUGS
The Addictive Personality
Escape from Anxiety and Stress
Getting Help *Treatments for Drug Abuse*
Treating Mental Illness
Teenage Depression and Drugs

HEROIN

THE ENCYCLOPEDIA OF PSYCHOACTIVE DRUGS

HEROIN

The Street Narcotic

FRED ZACKON, M.Ed.

GENERAL EDITOR (U.S.A.)
Professor Solomon H. Snyder, M.D.
*Distinguished Service Professor of Neuroscience, Pharmacology
and Psychiatry at
The Johns Hopkins University School of Medicine*

GENERAL EDITOR (U.K.)
Professor Malcolm H. Lader, D.Sc., Ph.D., M.D., F.R.C. Psych.
*Professor of Clinical Psychopharmacology
at the Institute of Psychiatry, University of London,
and Honorary Consultant to the Bethlem Royal and Maudsley
Hospitals*

Burke Publishing Company Limited
LONDON

First published in the United States of America 1986
© 1986 by Chelsea House Publishers,
a division of Chelsea House Educational Communications, Inc.
This edition first published 1988
New material contained in this edition
© Burke Publishing Company Limited 1988
All rights reserved. No part of this publication may be reproduced, stored in a retrieval system, or transmitted in any form or by any means, electronic, mechanical, photocopying, recording or otherwise, without the prior permission of Burke Publishing Company Limited.

Acknowledgements
Photos courtesy of AP/Wide Photos, Ardea, Central Office of Information – reproduced with the permission of the Controller, Her Majesty's Stationery Office, Eli Lily Company, *High Times,* National Library of Medicine, HM Customs and Excise, London Express News and Feature Services, *Newsweek, The New York Times,* Phoenix House, Susan Quist, Rockefeller University, Roxanne Laboratories, St Bartholomew's Hospital, *Time,* UPI/Bettmann Archive, Washington Post DC Public Library.

CIP data
Zackon, Fred
    Heroin (Encyclopedia of psychoactive drugs)
        1. Heroin—Psychological aspects 2. Heroin—Physiological effect
        I. Title. II. Series.
    615'.
ISBN 0 222 01211 0 Hardbound
ISBN 0 222 01211 9 Paperback

Burke Publishing Company Limited
Pegasus House, 116-120 Golden Lane, London EC1Y 0TL, England.
Printed in Spain, by Jerez Industrial, S.A.

CONTENTS

Introduction 7
1 Poppies and Populations: A Brief History 13
2 Heroin Addiction in the Modern World 41
3 How Heroin Affects Its Users 59
4 Theories of Heroin Addiction 77
5 The Challenge of Recovery 95
6 Treatment and Rehabilitation 103
Some Useful Addresses 120
Further Reading 122
Glossary 123
Index 126

A 17th-century engraving depicts a man in Eastern dress collecting opium juice from the buds of poppy plants. Opium's painkilling, calming, and sleep-inducing properties were probably recognized as early as 3300 BC.

INTRODUCTION

The late twentieth century has seen the rapid growth of both the legitimate medical use and the illicit, non-medical abuse of an increasing number of drugs which affect the mind. Both use and abuse are very high in general in the U.S.A. and great concern is voiced there. Other Western countries are not far behind and cannot afford to ignore the matter or to shrug off the consequent problems. Nevertheless, differences between countries may be marked and significant: they reflect such factors as social habits, economic status, attitude towards the young and towards drugs, and the ways in which health care is provided and laws are enacted and enforced.

Drug abuse particularly concerns the young but other age groups are not immune. Alcoholism in middle-aged men and increasingly in middle-aged women is one example, tranquillizers in women another. Even the old may become alcoholic or dependent on their barbiturates. And the most widespread form of addiction and the one with the most dire consequences to health is cigarette smoking.

Why do so many drug problems start in the teenage and even pre-teenage years? These years are critical in the human life-cycle as they involve maturation from child to adult. During these relatively few years adolescents face the difficult tasks of equipping themselves physically and intellectually for adulthood and of establishing goals that make adult life worthwhile while coping with the search for personal identity, assuming their sexual roles, and learning to come to terms with authority. During this intense period of

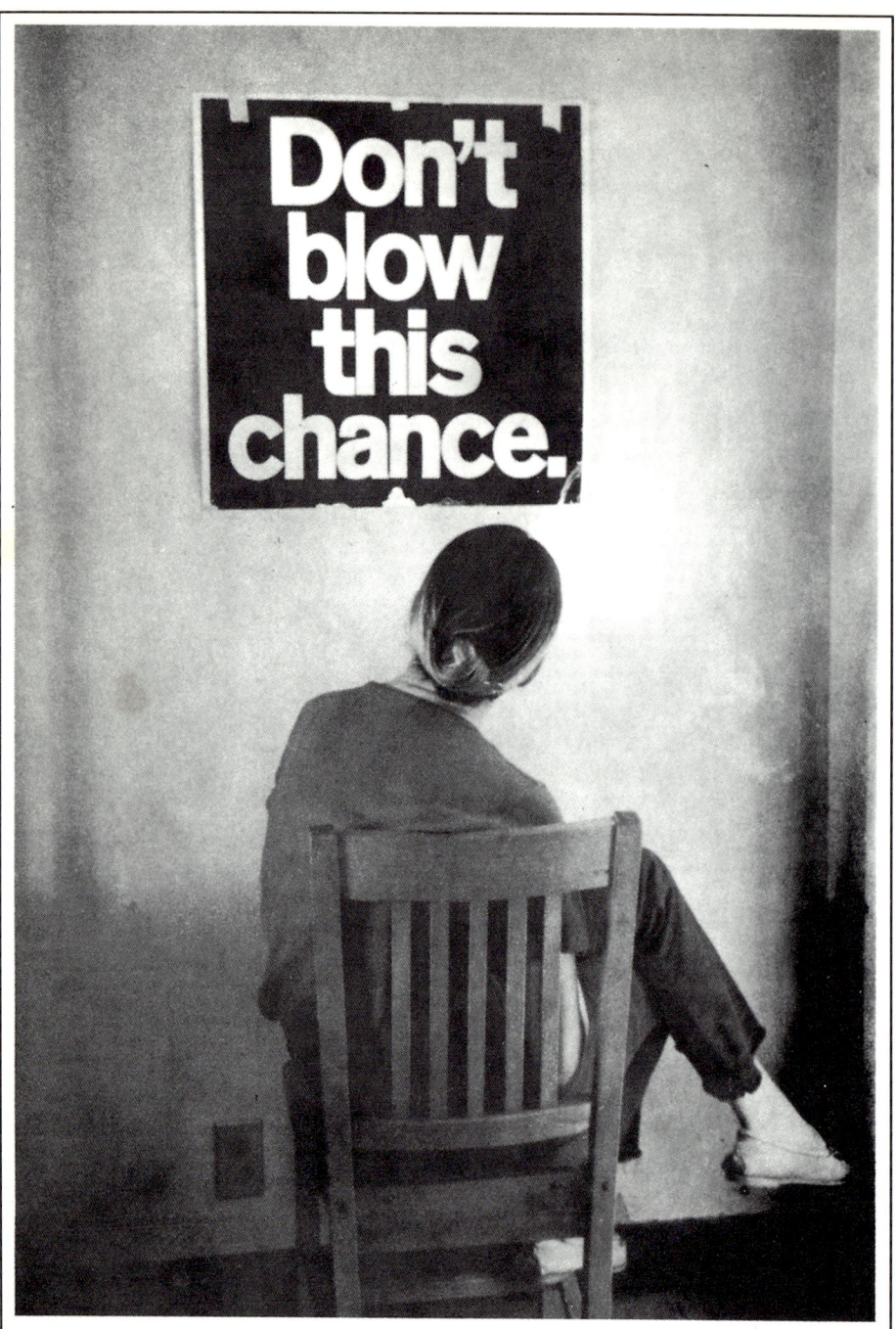

This woman sits alone facing a wall where she was told to sit by former narcotics addicts who run a treatment programme. The addict's desire to change is essential to a successful recovery from an opiate dependency.

growth and activity, bewilderment and conflict are inevitable, and peer pressure to experiment and to escape from life's apparent problems become overwhelming. Drugs are increasingly available and offer a tempting respite.

Unfortunately, the consequences may be serious. But the penalties for drug-taking must be put in perspective. Thus, addicts die from heroin addiction but people also die from alcoholism and even more from smoking-related diseases. Also, one must separate the direct effects of drug-taking from those indirectly related to the life-style of so many addicts. The problems of most addicts include many factors other than drug-taking itself. The chaotic existence or social deterioration of some may be the cause rather than the effect of drug abuse.

Drug use and abuse must be set into its social context. It reflects a complex interaction between the drug substance, naturally-occuring or synthetic, the person, psychologically normal or abnormal, and society, vigorous or sick. Fads affect drug-taking, as with most other human activities, with drugs being heavily abused one year and unfashionable the next. Such swings also typify society's response to drug abuse. Opiates were readily available in European pharmacies in the last century but are stringently controlled now. Marijuana is accepted and alcohol forbidden in many Islamic countries; the reverse obtains in most Western countries.

The use of psychoactive drugs dates back to prehistory. Opium was used in Ancient Egypt to alleviate pain; and its main constituent, morphine, remains a favoured drug for pain relief. Alcohol was incorporated into religious ceremonies in the cradles of civilization in the Near and Middle East and has been a focus of social activity ever since. Coca leaf has been chewed by the Andean Indians to lessen fatigue; and its modern derivative, cocaine, was used as a local anaesthetic. More recently, a succession of psychoactive drugs have been synthesized, developed and introduced into medicine to allay psychological distress and to treat psychiatric illness. But even so, these innovations may present unexpected problems such as the difficulties in stopping the long-term use of tranquillizers or slimming pills, even when taken under medical supervision.

The Encyclopedia Of Psychoactive Drugs provides information about the nature of the effects on mind and body of

The babies of mothers who are addicted to opiates are often born with a narcotics dependency themselves. Clara Hale, 79, runs a foster home to care for the infants of drug addicts.

alcohol and drugs and the possible results of abuse. Topics include where the drugs come from, how they are made, how they affect the body and how the body deals with these chemicals; the effects on the mind, thinking, emotions, the will and the intellect are detailed; the processes of use and abuse are discussed, as are the consequences for everyday activities such as school work, employment, driving, and dealing with other people. Pointers to identifying drug users and ways of helping them are provided. In particular, this series aims to dispel myths about drug-taking and to present the facts as objectively as possible without all the emotional distortion and obscurity which surrounds the subject. We seek neither to exaggerate nor to downplay the complex topics concerning various forms of drug abuse. We hope that young people will find answers to their questions and that others—parents and teachers for example—will also find the series helpful.

The series was originally written for American readers by American experts. Often the problem with a drug is particularly pressing in the USA or even largely confined to that country. We have invited a series of British experts to adapt the series for use in non-American English-speaking countries and believe that this widening of scope has successfully increased the relevance of these books to take account of the international drug scene.

Heroin is the street drug, par excellence. It remains the most favoured of this group of compounds—the "opioids". Its use has become widespread, mainly by inhalation—"chasing the magic dragon", but also by intravenous injection. An additional complication is the transmission of AIDS by the sharing of needles.

Nevertheless, recovery from heroin addiction is commonplace, both in terms of discontinuing usage and in the form of rehabilitation and the building of new and more rewarding lifestyles. In this book, the whole problem of heroin use is discussed in an informative and unemotional way. Treatment is emphasized, as is rehabilitation and prevention of relapse.

M. H. Lader

A pipe, scale, spirit lamp, and a violin-shaped case are all paraphernalia that can be used by opium smokers. On the other hand, heroin, a derivative of the opium poppy, is almost always taken by injection.

CHAPTER 1

POPPIES AND POPULATIONS: A BRIEF HISTORY

Heroin is a drug derived from the opium poppy, *Papaver somniferum,* which means "the poppy that brings sleep". This name, however, hardly describes the many ways in which the extracts from the poppy affect human beings.

Opium's calming, painkilling and sleep-inducing properties were first recognized more than 4,000 years ago and its use in medicine continues today. At one time, it was thought to bring courage to soldiers going into battle. Economies and trade routes were based on opium supply, and wars between nations in the East and West were fought because of it. Poets claiming to have gained visionary powers from opium have composed rich and lyrical verse. The accounts of opium users, however, also reveal the great suffering, unbearable addiction and death caused by this powerful drug. Bold and often unsound claims, in the guise of scientific fact, have often been made about opium.

First synthesized in 1898 from morphine (a drug derived from opium), heroin was thought to be a safe means of curtailing or curing morphine addiction. In fact, Bayer, the company known for manufacturing aspirin, gave its version of the new product the name Heroin and began an intense, though brief, marketing campaign near the end of the 19th century. Heroin was included in medicines such as cough suppressants and its potential for abuse was largely ignored.

It was many years before civil and medical authorities began to control the drug's distribution. This is because the economics of opium and its highly publicized and, to some degree, successful use in medicine (for example, to induce sleep in babies who have colic, or stomach irritation, and to bring relief from intense pain) coloured people's perception of the drug, as did a number of naive theories and claims about the nature of heroin addiction. Since then a great deal of scientific data has accumulated, and today it is known that addiction to heroin has caused and continues to cause tremendous misery around the world.

The Early Use of Opium

Archaeological evidence suggests that more than 5,000 years ago in Mesopotamia (the area that is now Iraq), the Sumerians treated many ills with medicines made from the poppy. Later, the Assyrians and then the Babylonians inherited the art of slitting the flowering bulb of the poppy plant to collect and dry the milky juices, using the seed capsules to prepare potions. The ancient Egyptians called their opium preparations *thebacium* because the highly potent poppies used to make them grew near the capital city of Thebes. Egyptian priest physicians praised the magic of the poppy and its household use spread throughout their civilization. The poppy's importance was so great that pharaohs were even entombed with opium artifacts at their sides. When Egyptian and Phoenician traders sailed across the Mediterranean to Greece and Rome, they brought the mysterious poppy with them. Often regarded as a gift of the gods, opium was mentioned in many myths and epics from these ancient cultures.

Hippocrates, the Greek physician who is generally recognized as the father of modern medicine, was one of the first people to describe the medicinal use of opium. He prescribed it frequently, and thereby helped establish practices that doctors would follow for 2,400 years. Galen, a Greek physician who practised in the Roman Empire in the 2nd century, standardized the preparation of opium, creating a recipe called *mithridate.*

The poppy is technically a herb. White- or purple-petalled, the opium poppy is difficult to cultivate and grows best in moderate or warm climates. The process of collecting and preparing the plant's gummy juices is quite laborious. For these reasons, ancient peoples either ate parts of the flower or made them into liquids for drinking. By the 7th century, the Turkish and Islamic cultures of western Asia, however, had discovered that the drug's most powerful effects were produced by igniting and smoking the poppy's congealed juices. The Turks succeeded in cultivating larger crops. Arab merchants, who traded with peoples in the Far East, provided an economic incentive for the Turkish poppy cultivation by introducing the plant into these new markets. People in India and China soon began drinking or eating mild opium potions to ease the pain of minor ailments.

As early as the 11th century, Islamic doctors, the most advanced physicians of the pre-modern world, noted that the more opium a person took, the more he or she needed to take to gain the same effects experienced previously (an indication that an individual's body has become *tolerant* to the effects of the drug). By the 14th century, Arab scientists observed that continued use of the drug "degenerates", "corrupts", and "weakens the mind". It was already common knowledge that a single overdose could lead to death.

In Europe, opium use declined under the strong influence of the medieval Catholic church, which had strict doctrines

The ancient Greek physician Hippocrates, one of the first people to write about a medicinal use for opium, established practices that doctors would follow for well over 2,000 years. Hippocrates argued that diet, lifestyle and environment should be considered when treating illness.

about medicine. Then, in the early 16th century, Paracelsus, a brilliant and unconventional Swiss physician and chemist, created a concoction known as laudanum, whose principal ingredient was opium. Paracelsus claimed that the drug could cure, not just ease, any pain-producing disease. He even insisted that laudanum could rejuvenate those who were close to death. Paracelsus and his followers attracted wide attention, and throughout the Western world laudanum gradually became one of the most popular and abused medications of all time. Even so, in Europe the availability of strong opium was limited until the 18th century, when increases in trade ushered in a new era.

The Growth of Opium Use

Authorized by the British Crown to advance English trade in India and the Far East, the British East India Company, a private commercial firm, began to make huge profits as the popularity of opium grew throughout southeastern Asia. In

The physician Galen, appointed to care for the Roman gladiators, was a follower of Hippocratic theories of medicine and treated his patients with a preparation of opium called mithridate.

some ways, the British merely brought new life to a well-established market originally created by the Arab traders. In fact, by the time the Europeans arrived in India in the 16th century, in some cities "Take your opium" was a standard greeting.

Strongly held religious beliefs and cultural values in India were in conflict with the widespread use and frequent abuse of opium. But the appeal of the drug was so great that for millions of people in the Far East it proved irresistible—a fact that was not lost upon powerful Western companies. The Chinese imperial court vacillated over whether and how to control the growing use of opium, and it was no match for the aggressive traders who were supplying the drug.

During the 18th century, the British acquired an opium habit of their own. Ships from India supplied chemists and pharmacists all over Great Britain with literally tonnes of the drug. Countless varieties of new opium-based wonder drugs appeared everywhere, as did all kinds of publications that praised their virtues. The opium suppliers and merchants were hard at work in a riotous free market, each promoting his own supposedly superior products. As the 18th century drew to a close, one or more of the competing opium products could be found in virtually every British home.

There were doctors and scientists who could see the dangers of the excessive use of opium, but it was difficult to document social health problems at that time, so the dangers went unpublicized. The result was that neither the general public nor the authorities saw much cause for concern. Unlike alcohol, which even the ancient Romans knew could produce an uncontrollable and sometimes deadly craving in its users, opium was seen as a medicine. The very idea of addiction to a "cure" lacked a scientific basis in the biological and psychological theories of the day. Moreover, many of the people most actively investigating opium—doctors and chemists—were themselves frequent consumers of the drug. As a result, unbiased opinions on the issue were hard to come by.

Also, the government itself had a large stake in the continued consumption of opium, since taxes on Indian exports and domestic imports accounted for a sizable part of British revenues. Opium, therefore, remained a cheap, plentiful and readily available drug.

"Gods Own Medicine"

Having observed how poppy extracts varied greatly in their strength, Frederick Sertuerner, a German scientist, was determined to isolate the "specific narcotic elements of opium". In 1803 he derived from opium a crystal *alkaloid* (an organic compound that contains nitrogen) so potent that astonishingly small amounts produced powerful effects. Remembering Morpheus, the Greek god of dreams and sleep, Sertuerner called this chemical morphine. Within 20 years, morphine would begin to change the practice of medicine more quickly and dramatically than even opium had. And just as dramatically, it would transform the experience of drug addiction.

These transformations were made possible by the invention and refinement of the hypodermic syringe during the 1840s and 1850s. This device made it possible to administer morphine by injection, which guaranteed that the drug would be quickly absorbed into the bloodstream. As a result doctors—and, shortly thereafter, drug addicts—learned that injections into the veins brought extremely rapid and intense responses. Because injecting morphine required a degree of experience and skill, initially the practice was restricted to doctors, who were rapturous over the painkilling properties of the new drug. One leading British doctor went so far as to proclaim morphine "Gods own medicine". By the middle of the 19th century morphine was being widely used throughout Europe and the United States to ease every kind of discomfort. In fact, the sales of this one drug helped establish some of the world's leading drug companies.

Amidst the enthusiasm, however, there were new warnings: the personal accounts of sadder but wiser opiate addicts. (The term opiate refers to the entire family of poppy-based drugs.) Although a century later there would be a cascade of such tales, the most celebrated account was that of the British writer Thomas de Quincey. His book, *Confessions of an English Opium-Eater,* published in 1822, engrossed both medical professionals and the reading public. It is the intimate narration of how his own medicinal use of laudanum was transformed into a euphoric pastime that went on to become a raging nightmare. The *Confessions* documented the phenomena of tolerance (how the use of a few drops of even a mild opiate tincture could swell to the need for much larger amounts of the substance); denial (how a chronic user would deceive him or herself about the escalating abuse and dependence); and withdrawal (the unbearable agonies brought on by the cessation of drug use). Inadvertently, de Quincey also opened the door to the use of laudanum and other opiates by authors and poets during the 19th century, including Samuel Taylor Coleridge, Charles Baudelaire, Lord Byron, John Keats, Edgar Allan Poe, Elizabeth Barrett Browning, and Algernon Swinburne. But although they and other artists sometimes searched for creativity through opium, most 19th-century artists took the drug in the way that almost everyone did—as medicine. Pharmacies sold little vials of laudanum (and even candied opiates later in the century) by the thousands. It was cheaper than gin. The working class, the very young, the very old—nearly everyone took laudanum.

The Opium Wars

The big business of opium continued to thrive in the East. The habit of smoking raw opium had made its way up from India along the southeastern coast of China. Native poppy cultivation was also spreading. Although the British population enjoyed opium as a gift, the guardians of China's culture saw that opium wasted the lives of its smokers. It cost their

In the 19th century the British aggressively marketed India-grown opium. The quality, price and destination of this crop were determined by men with strong commercial interests and expertise.

nation silver and other trade commodities that it could ill afford, and it humbled the ancient Central Kingdom (as China was then called) before the mercenary West. (The West included the Americans who, to the great displeasure of the British, smuggled Turkish opium into China.) The smoke from opium dens, where users gathered to enjoy their pipes in secret, drifted over the coastlines and even rose above inland cities. Even the emperor's court had its smokers, as did all levels within the government and the army. By 1820 more than 300 tonnes of pure opium were imported annually. Ten years later, even after officials attempted harsh restrictions, the figure approached 2,000 tonnes a year. It is estimated that millions of Chinese were addicted to opium.

The British government was still convinced that more

The hypodermic syringe, invented in the mid-1800s, revolutionized medical practice because it allowed precise administration of a drug by injection, resulting in quick absorption into the bloodstream.

profit was possible from the opium traders. It revoked the charter of the British East India Company and acted directly to open Chinese ports to even more opium trade. The Chinese emperor was under strong pressure from his advisers to legalize opium. Although opium was still considered unsafe, the authorities hoped that through legislation, corruption and foreign influence could be minimized. But the emperor refused to legalize the drug. Instead, he began military preparations and ordered the executions of users and traffickers, foreign and domestic. The most notable effect of this policy was to anger the British. Within a year, the Opium War of 1839 began. When the Chinese lost the war, three years later, they were forced to sign the Treaty of Nanking, which required them to pay large reparations and to surrender totally to British commercial interests. As a result, by 1852 opium imports had doubled. In 1856, with China under the rule of a new emperor, a second opium war began. This, however, brought China only more death, more reparations to pay and more humiliation. Opium became officially legalized, and the Chinese ports were opened as never before to Western influences of every sort.

The Opium Wars have generated much analysis and historical commentary. Today, many historians believe that opportunistic commercial interests had merely taken advantage of opium as a commodity—an especially insidious one to be sure—seeking any way to attain financial success. The clash between the expanding industrial powers of the West and the protective, tradition-bound culture of China might well have erupted eventually over some other commodity.

A Dope Fiend's Paradise

In the United States during this period, as in Britain, laudanum and similar opiate tinctures (alcohol extracts) had become popular home remedies. Americans were even less inclined than the British to see opium's potential dangers. Indeed, between 1830 and 1870, when the land was awash with patent medicines, the United States' importation of opium increased twentyfold.

During the 1850s and 1860s tens of thousands of Chinese entered the United States to help build the western railways and to work the California mines. They brought with them the practice of opium smoking. Besides being an integral part of Chinese lifestyle, opium smoking provided some measure of relief from the dirty, unhealthy and physically demanding work they performed. Thus, the United States came to know Chinese opium smoking firsthand as the opium dens of the West Coast became steadily more common and notorious.

Shortly after the Civil War, West Coast authorities, influenced by strong racist sentiments, enacted the nation's first anti-opium laws. The public's grossly distorted image of the addict was that of the predatory, godless and depraved Oriental. One consequence of this view was that the public failed to recognize addiction among its white citizens, who never visited the Chinese "dens of iniquity" or smoked opium, but were addicted in other ways.

Further changing the course of opium use in the United States and abroad was the use of morphine—as both a painkiller and to combat dysentery—during times of war. Particularly in the American Civil War, and to a lesser extent in the European wars later in the 19th century, morphine was used so freely on the battlefield that its over-use became known as the "army disease". Only when many Civil War veterans became obviously dependent on morphine did American society as a whole suddenly become more familiar with the drug.

However, it was not just soldiers and patent medicine salesmen who spread the word about morphine's "miraculous" properties. In 1868 one of the country's leading medical textbooks described opiates in the following glowing terms:

> *[opiates] cause a feeling of delicious ease and comfort, with an elevation and expansion of the whole moral and intellectual nature. . . . There is not the same uncontrollable excitement as from alcohol, but an exaltation of our better mental qualities, a warmer glow of benevolence, a disposition to do great things, but nobly and beneficently, a higher devotional spirit and withal a stronger self-reliance and consciousness of power. Nor is this consciousness altogether mistaken. For the intellectual and imaginative faculties are raised to the highest point compati-*

ble with individual capacity.... Opium seems to make the individual, for a time, a better and greater man.

Who could resist such a "medicine"? And why *would* anyone resist it? Opiates were legal, abundant and cheap. The mystery of how they actually worked within the body continued to evoke only vague and colourful speculation. Public opinion held that only people who were constitutionally weak in body and mind needed to abstain from opiates. As the last years of the 19th century approached, the United States was, in the words of one historian, a "dope fiend's paradise".

Changing Perceptions and New Realities

While opiates and other drugs (such as cocaine) were

Portrait of Thomas de Quincey, author of **Confessions of an English Opium-Eater.** *First published in 1822, and still in print, de Quincey's book tells of the unbearable agonies brought on by attempts to end a drug addiction.*

beginning to cause serious trouble in the United States, Britain's relatively stable society was being affected by a more moderate drug-consumption problem. Although there was not a large addict population in Britain, there was a pervasive, low level addiction to laudanum-type medicines, a problem that was seen as largely "medical". As British anti-opium groups began to agitate more strongly for reform at home as well as abroad, the sale of opiate products increasingly became restricted to pharmacies. At the same time, British moral reform groups, often led by overseas missionaries, were also becoming more aware of the opium problems in China and India. They expressed outrage and guilt about the Opium Wars and demanded an end to the opium trade. Slowly, opiate use among the British began to decrease.

In the United States there was a different atmosphere that contributed to an unprecedented increase in the abuse of

An engraving depicts an 1842 battle during the Opium War between China and Britain. Fearing the devastating effects of opium on his people, the Chinese emperor fought a losing battle to stop its importation.

opiates. Between 1880 and 1910 the US population grew by 83%. Personal liberty was romanticized and often zealously guarded. Economic and social progress seemed to promise an end to all known ills and suffering. New fashions travelled from coast to coast at unheard-of speed, and there was a great desire to be up to date. One of the most up-to-date fashions was opiate use, and the amount of imported opium rose dramatically during the late 1800s. During this period, in Iowa alone, a state still relatively free of opium dens and big-city vices, sales of over-the-counter opiated medicines jumped by 700%. In 1883 such products were sold in more than 3,000 stores. In its 1897 mail-order catalogue, Sears, Roebuck and Company then offered a selection of hypodermic syringe kits. An individual could easily obtain morphine at any pharmacy, and a few years later, heroin became available. By 1906 there were 50,000 different patent medicines containing opiates.

The principal consumers of patent medicines were middle- and upper-class people, mainly older women in the northeast and white males in the south. Many customers took these remedies on a regular high-dose basis; others consumed low doses of relatively mild formulas constantly over long periods, apparently without ill effects. But among many people in every walk of life there began to appear some classic symptoms: insomnia, moodiness, depression, loss of concentration, chronic constipation, an obsessive need for one's "medicine", and intense physical illness whenever drug use was abruptly discontinued.

In newspapers, popular magazines and professional journals, sensationalized personal stories of the horror of addiction began to appear. Yet many doctors continued to praise and prescribe narcotics. Others, however, were quicker to notice the telltale signs of addiction and began to write about "morphinism", "narcomania", and the "disease" of the "opium appetite". Administering morphine by injection warranted special concern. One eminent physician wrote, "There is no proceeding in medicine that has become so rapidly popular...so great a blessing, and so great a curse". Opiate addiction in the United States was becoming all too obvious. In 1920 New York City officials reported that in their city alone 300,000 people were "hooked" on morphine or the new scourge, heroin.

Public awareness of the problem came slowly and unevenly. Many newspapers in the western United States blamed the relatively small population of Chinese labourers for spreading addiction. Sensationalist "yellow journalism" and racism were used to publicize the issue. Even the progressive labour leader Samuel Gompers, "Father of American Labour Unions", wrote emotional tracts that linked opium smoking and "coolie" (Chinese) labour to a coming social catastrophe. He wrote about American youths who had to "yield up their virgin bodies to their maniacal yellow captors" and said that "our American girls and boys who have acquired this deathly habit opium-smoking are doomed, hopelessly doomed". In reality, the boom-and-bust conditions in San Francisco and other western cities where the Chinese lived had generated all the gambling, prostitution and other forms of vice necessary to attract wayward youths.

For a while, cannabis (then usually called hashish) and cocaine were also used in some patent medicines. But neither drug had the established market or the unique medical value of opium. After 1900, their use seemed to be more common among southern Blacks, bohemian Whites, and others who often found themselves either in conflict with or the targets of conventional attitudes. These groups helped to establish the networks through which opiates would flow most easily in later years. Like the Chinese, these groups were easy targets and thus became the scapegoats for the social hostility that went hand-in-hand with the 20th-century attack on all drugs.

In the United States in the late 1800s, moral reform movements provided the momentum for a revised attitude to drugs. Religious fundamentalist groups sought to preserve pre-Civil War values and social norms against the incursions of industrialization and the influence of new immigrants and freed slaves. Progressive reformers spoke out against corruption in politics and big business. And the temperance movement's crusade against "demon" alcohol was gaining in importance. These various movements had a great influence on American society, and gradually their moralistic messages began to include anti-opiate sentiments.

In 1898, as one of the spoils of the Spanish-American War, the United States acquired the Philippines and thus became the protector of a large population that included many opium users. Just as England had a foreign drug problem, the United States now had one too. In addition, many Americans believed that soldiers sent to the Philippines risked becoming addicted. Calls for controls on the distribution of opium were sounded as nations around the world came to see how difficult it was to limit use of the drug.

Meanwhile, a new drug appeared on the scene. In 1874 the British chemist C. R. Wright synthesized diacetylmorphine from morphine. But the substance did not become known to doctors or the general public in the United States until almost 25 years later. In 1898 Heinrich Dreser, a chemist who helped develop aspirin, also synthesized diacetylmorphine. Dreser, however, was backed by his employer, the Bayer Company. Finding the new medicine more potent than morphine, and apparently less apt to produce nausea,

An opium den in New York City's Chinatown. Opiate addiction had become a serious problem by the 1920s, and many Americans unjustly blamed the small Chinese population for its use.

constipation and the other side effects of the opiates, Bayer promoted it as a singularly effective cough suppressant. Soon, however, company researchers discovered that this new drug produced the same dependence that was associated with morphine. In fact, diacetylmorphine did so more quickly than any other opiate. Bayer immediately stopped promoting diacetylmorphine, but continued to distribute it. Although the drug never became a stock item on store shelves, it remained legally available for a generation. This was enough time for much less sophisticated laboratories around the world to learn how to reproduce Wright's and Dreser's new medicine and make famous the trade name Bayer had given it—heroin.

Attempts to Cure and Control Opiate Addiction

Opiate addiction was officially recognized as early as the 11th century. Cures that involved alchemy, sorcery and herbal antidotes were all attempted, but none achieved any notable success. Not surprisingly, as addiction increased in the 19th

The extensive administration of morphine as both a painkiller and a relief for dysentery during the American Civil War altered the patterns of opium use throughout the rest of the 19th century.

century the search for a cure gained momentum. But the question remained: Who needed to be cured, and of what exactly were they to be cured? Most users of mildly opiated home remedies showed no ill effects as long as they had enough of their "medicine". The popular view was that there were really two kinds of addicts. The first type was the deviant who, because he or she belonged to an "inferior" race and/or had a defective personality, took drugs as a wicked pleasure, with little concern for the consequences. The second type of addict was the good but unfortunate citizen whose problems were a result of unintentional overuse of medicinal opiates. This distinction, reinforced by the press and other organizations, was entirely misleading and disguised the true nature of addiction.

Another popular misconception was that discontinuing opiate use could lead directly to death. Although most doctors knew this outcome was unlikely and, in fact, almost unheard of, when they encountered a patient whose habit was out of control, they rarely advised abstinence. Instead, they would recommend some other opiate that they considered safer or administer other drugs such as belladonna.

Belladonna, known since ancient times as a herbal medicine extracted from the poisonous plant *Atropa belladonna*, is a non-addicting but very powerful mood-altering tranquillizer that affects the central nervous system. The chemicals in belladonna were thought to help purge opiates from the stomach and the intestinal tract. This purge therapy was supported by contemporary theories that addiction would end if the body could be fully rid of opiate "toxins", or poisons. By the turn of the century, throughout the United States and Europe, purge therapy had become a big business.

Countless quicker, cheaper and less painful "cures" were also highly popular. Most of these were simply disguised opiates that allowed addicts to think, at least for a day or so, that their *detoxification* (a gradual to rapid weaning from opiate use), had been painless. There were also claims that other remedies, including largely unaided withdrawals in confined sanitariums, were successful. "Cure clinics" reported that 90% of their patients were completely withdrawn from drugs.

Such encouraging assertions, however, could not be

supported by hard facts. In fact, most patients, even those who had gone to the most "successful" sanitariums, ended up returning to opiate use, usually within six months of their "cure". Even addicts who were desperate for a cure often readmitted themselves to clinics because they could not stay away from opiates. Scientists did not understand why this behaviour pattern occurred. They discovered no toxins or chemical clues that could explain the relapses. Doctors were at a loss and could recommend only continued moderate use of opiates. For the "bad" addicts, who did not seek medical help (which frequently only the wealthy could afford), even harder times were to come.

Cure specialists continued to promote their techniques with great energy. In addition, the belief that cures were available convinced American lawmakers that opiates could be used safely if their distribution was restricted. With San Francisco taking the lead in enacting local ordinances, in the 1870s California and the other western states began to limit the sale of raw opium and enacted other measures, usually pointedly anti-Chinese, to prohibit opium-smoking. In 1883 and again in 1890, the United States Congress raised the tariffs on opium prepared for smoking, and in 1909 it completely banned the importation of opium. Unfortunately, as a result, drug smuggling and illicit distribution increased. Newly formed criminal organizations, called "tongs" in the Chinese community, trafficked in opium and, in the process caused an unprecedented degree of corruption and violence.

The drug companies and their merchandisers fought to keep processed opiates available. They did, however, conform to the federal Pure Food and Drug Act of 1906, which required that opiated patent medicines carry labels listing their ingredients. Informed about what their remedies really contained, many Americans chose to reduce their opiate consumption sharply.

Sparked by President Theodore Roosevelt's anti-narcotics adviser, Dr Hamilton Wright, the first of two international conferences was held in Shanghai in 1909. Out of this conference came a statement regarding the Western concern about opium addiction in China and the vow of all conference participants to begin a worldwide effort to restrict the distribution of narcotics. The second conference, The Hague Convention of 1912, made specific recommendations to further the goals announced in Shanghai.

These gatherings further spurred the efforts of US authorities to solve their country's own opiate problems. In 1914 Congress passed the Harrison Act. On the surface a tax on opiates, it actually sought to restrict dramatically the distribution of narcotics and cocaine (but *not* heroin, which Congress did not yet know to be addictive) and limit even doctors' prescribing powers.

The Heroin Addict as Criminal

The Harrison Act, along with a host of similar laws, judicial rulings, and enforcement practices, brought rapid decreases both in the consumption of opiates in the United States and in the number of consumers. As a consequence, the incidence of new addictions was also reduced. These laws also caused tens of thousands of people who were only marginally addicted to stop using opiates. The impact on true opiate addiction, however, was another matter. The authorities who promoted the Harrison Act believed that there were cures for

An 1862 photograph of the ambulance corps that was organized shortly after the Battle of Antietam. Morphine was prescribed so freely during the Civil War that its overdose became known as the "army disease".

addiction; but, in fact, these "cures" usually consisted only of detoxification and were available only to those who could afford to enter private clinics. As a result, most detoxified individuals relapsed within months, and poorer addicts were seldom treated at all. In addition, within a year after New York State banned other opiates in 1913, almost all the addicts in New York City had turned to heroin. With the imposition of the Harrison Act, a similar phenomenon occurred nationwide.

Chemically more potent and, to many addicts, more euphoric than morphine, heroin did not need to be injected; a user could snort, or sniff, it. Congress finally became aware of the problem, and in 1924 federal law made the use of heroin illegal.

The criminalization of opiates had far-ranging social

An engraving depicts an anti-Chinese riot during the 1880s. During this era, the Chinese were the victims of severe and sometimes violent racism. They were accused of being the only group that smoked opium; this convenient delusion allowed white citizens to ignore the drug addiction that was rampant within their own community.

consequences. Indeed, in 1919 the United States Supreme Court ruled that the Harrison Act forbade even doctors from authorizing long-term, or maintenance, doses for deeply dependent users—no matter what the origin of the dependence was. So vigorous was the enforcement effort that within 10 years of its formation, the Bureau of Narcotics had arrested 25,000 doctors and twice as many drug users. The old distinction between "good" and "bad" addicts was rapidly breaking down.

Public anti-narcotics campaigns stressed the criminality of addiction, claiming that heroin was "the most crime-inspiring of all drugs" and that its users became "insane" and "bloodthirsty". Caught up in the pervasive fear of foreign powers and internal subversives that existed during the period surrounding World War I, American politicians, newspaper editors, veterans' organizations, local police and countless other voices of "patriotism" and "order" spread the rumour that "dope fiends" (heroin addicts) brought anarchy and sedation, were enslaved by the "German invention", were Bolsheviks (communists) and constituted a national menace.

The idea that heroin itself inspired crime or that it was the drug prefered by hardened criminals had little basis in fact. What *was* true was that during the same period when heroin was replacing other opiates, addicts were beginning to be prosecuted for the use and possession of drugs. The addict population was also becoming younger and more urban. The suppliers could now operate most profitably in the cities and, as opiates were now viewed as a forbidden and alluring vice of the adult world, more young people began to use drugs. City youth gangs were growing. They tended to attract young men who were newcomers to the city, often unemployed and disillusioned, burdened with large amounts of free time and eager for some excitement. Racist stereotypes of addicts returned once again, but this time the Blacks rather than the Chinese were the targets. Many misinformed people thought Blacks, who had already been unfairly linked with cocaine abuse and its consequences, were very likely to rape and assault under the influence of heroin.

New criminal organizations appeared and replaced the Chinese tongs' role in drug-trafficking. They owed their existence in part to Prohibition—the 18th Amendment to the

US Constitution, passed in 1919—which made alcoholic beverages illegal in the United States and inadvertently made bootlegging (the illegal production or sale of alcohol) a very big business. Although it would be years before the bootleggers would turn their attention from alcohol to heroin (Prohibition, a failed experiment, was finally repealed in 1933), the black market in narcotics was already taking shape by the 1920s. Using the black market as one's source of heroin meant paying much higher prices, depending on an uncertain supply, using adulterated drugs (drugs mixed with impurities), and dealing with unsavory associates—all of which made addiction a more desperate and dangerous lifestyle.

Recognizing that help was needed, between 1919 and 1920 the federal government authorized several dozen outpatient clinics in cities across the country to "cure" addicts who had no other resources. The addicts were detoxified through daily decreasing doses of morphine or heroin. Bitter controversies erupted surrounding charges that the clinics were *maintaining,* not detoxifying, their patients, and that

Trade unions in the United States, fearful of competing against cheap Chinese labour, supported restrictions against Chinese immigration during the 1870s and 1880s. This cartoon warns cigar makers not to use Chinese labour.

several facilities were poorly controlled and corruptly managed. Within a year, this notable effort at government-sponsored treatment was stopped, and all the clinics were forced to close. As a result, their 15,000 patients (and all the other addicts around the country) were left with few choices. If they could afford a doctor's services, they could get professional help; otherwise they either detoxified on their own or remained on the streets, where they continued to buy and use illegal drugs, a practice that frequently led to arrest and imprisonment, illness, or death from an overdose.

Different, more moderate trends continued in Great Britain. Controls on the importation of narcotics had steadily reduced the supply, and the medical profession had kept effective primary authority over the dispensing of opiates. In 1926 the Rolleston Report reaffirmed the long-held British position that "with few exceptions, addiction to morphine and heroin should be regarded as a manifestation of a morbid (that is, diseased) state and not as a mere form of vicious indulgence". Indeed, for the next 40 years the street addict who would come to loom so large on the American scene was rare in Great Britain, where most addicts received morphine on doctors' orders and under close medical supervision. Only in the 1960s did Britain once again have serious problems with illegal opiates and other drugs. By then, other Europeans were also confronting widespread narcotics abuse.

In Britain, a system was adopted whereby addicts were required to be notified to the Home Office by medical practitioners. The numbers of opiate addicts remained small until the 1960s and the problem was largely managed by the medical prescription of opiates (usually heroin) to such people. Within the British sociocultural context during the first half of the century, this controversial approach was found to work well.

In the 20th century, the Far East has had even greater success than the West battling with its opiate problem. Strong internal and international pressures brought an end to the large-scale importation of opium into China. And, though addiction and associated corruption continued into the 1930s, as national concerns they were overshadowed by the military and political upheavals of this revolutionary period. Mao Zedong's People's Republic of China brought a drastic conclusion to what remained of the old opium culture.

India, for so long the major grower of high-quality poppies, managed a particularly benign control and reduction of the opium supply. However, addiction rates had always remained relatively low in India, at least partly because of British supervision of cultivation and the traditional practice of using mild opiates primarily for medicinal and culturally approved purposes. As Indians assumed greater authority, and eventually achieved self-rule in 1947, they worked systematically and successfully to reduce both the cultivation and the use of opium by promoting traditional religious and moral values, which opposed intoxication. By the time Europe and America saw the use of heroin resurfacing among the young, addiction was nearly extinct in India, where the few opium addicts still living were mainly middle-aged or older. The decreased use of opiates in India and China began before either nation had significant exposure to morphine or heroin.

The American "dope fiend" began to fade from the headlines during the 1920s and the 1930s. Although the Bureau of Narcotics reported that its efforts had decreased drug use in fact addiction was merely becoming more covert—addicts were forced to remain underground and more frequently indentified by the crimes they had to commit to pay for heroin. Heroin was the perfect black-market drug because it was much easier and much more profitable to refine it overseas and ship small bags of its odourless powder through customs than it was to smuggle in large cargoes of raw, odorous opium. Because local distribution rings needed to avoid detection, they began to operate principally in poorer sections of large cities, where secret deals with the poor, young, urban drug-users could be made most easily. Only those addicts who had special connections or who were medical professionals managed to avoid the life of the heroin underworld. (There were more than a few addicts in both categories. Among the medical professionals was Dr William Halsted who, though a secret and heavy morphine addict until his death, was a pioneer in modern surgery and helped establish the Johns Hopkins Medical School.)

Although heroin addicts were popularly portrayed as wilful criminals, there were still doctors who were determined to discover a real cure—some way to end addiction other than by cutting off the supply of narcotics, which was rarely successful. In 1935 Congress allowed a new kind of corrections programme to start in Lexington, Kentucky. At that facility, which was a large, farmlike complex, convicted addicts were to be studied carefully and humanely and, as a pressing practical matter, admitted in numbers large enough to partially relieve the overburdened federal prisons. At the Addiction Research Centre component of the new facility, doctors and scientists would for the first time be able to apply systematic research to the phenomenon of opiate addiction. Treatment included gradual detoxification using morphine and, for several months thereafter, voluntary psychiatric counselling and work training. Although the

In many cities in the western United States, Chinese labourers were blamed for corrupting American youth. Chinese immigrants were thoroughly searched for opium when they arrived in San Francisco.

centre never claimed a cure rate of more than 15% through the 1950s its many distinguished researchers produced innovative studies of the physiology, psychology and behaviour of addiction. These studies form the basis of many present-day treatment techniques and current understanding about morphine.

Ironically, but not for the first time, treatment research produced new addicting drugs. The Lexington centre, in its search for new, safe painkillers, synthesized opiatelike substances that would eventually become widely prescribed by doctors and widely abused by both hard-core heroin addicts and less experienced users.

In the United States during the middle part of this century, the drug problem seemed to be relatively well contained. And in most of the rest of the world there were few dramatic changes or developments. World War II disrupted smuggling operations and diverted most opium to the medical needs of war victims all over the globe.

After World War II, heroin addiction was seen by most people as a problem which was largely confined to certain "fringe" groups in society, among them jazz musicians, bohemian artists, prostitutes, urban Blacks (in America) and criminal psychopaths. Most such groups were relegated to the underworld of polite society that no "decent" citizen

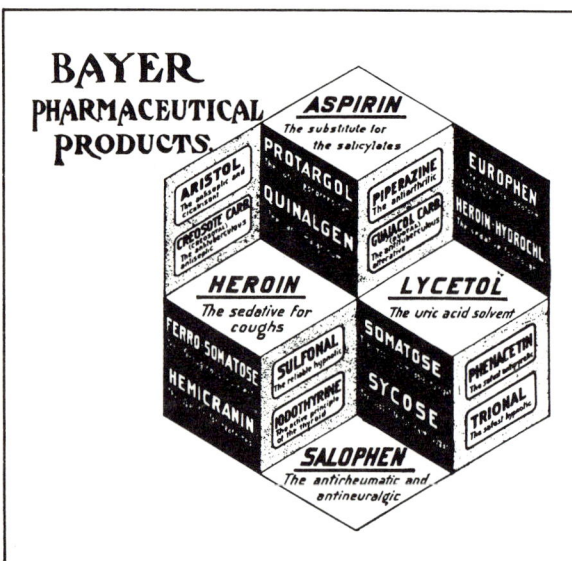

At the turn of the century, countless varieties of new "wonder drugs" appeared everywhere accompanied by extravagant and invalid claims about their effectiveness. By 1906 there were some 50,000 different brands of opiated formulas on the American market alone.

would want or need to enter. Such characterizations served to keep addicts and addiction at a safe mental distance. However, there were subtle and unnoticed changes going on in many societies during the late 1950s and early 1960s which were to prepare the way for later developments in the abuse of drugs.

In the 1960s, the youthful counter-culture swept the Western world. It was a time of unconventional fashions and anti-establishment attitudes. In unprecedented numbers, middle- and upper-class people experimented with illegal drugs to get high including derivatives of the opium poppy.

This 1903 advertisement for Glyco-Heroin promotes the medicinal properties that were ascribed to heroin. Some people mistakenly believed that the drug was also a cure for morphine addiction.

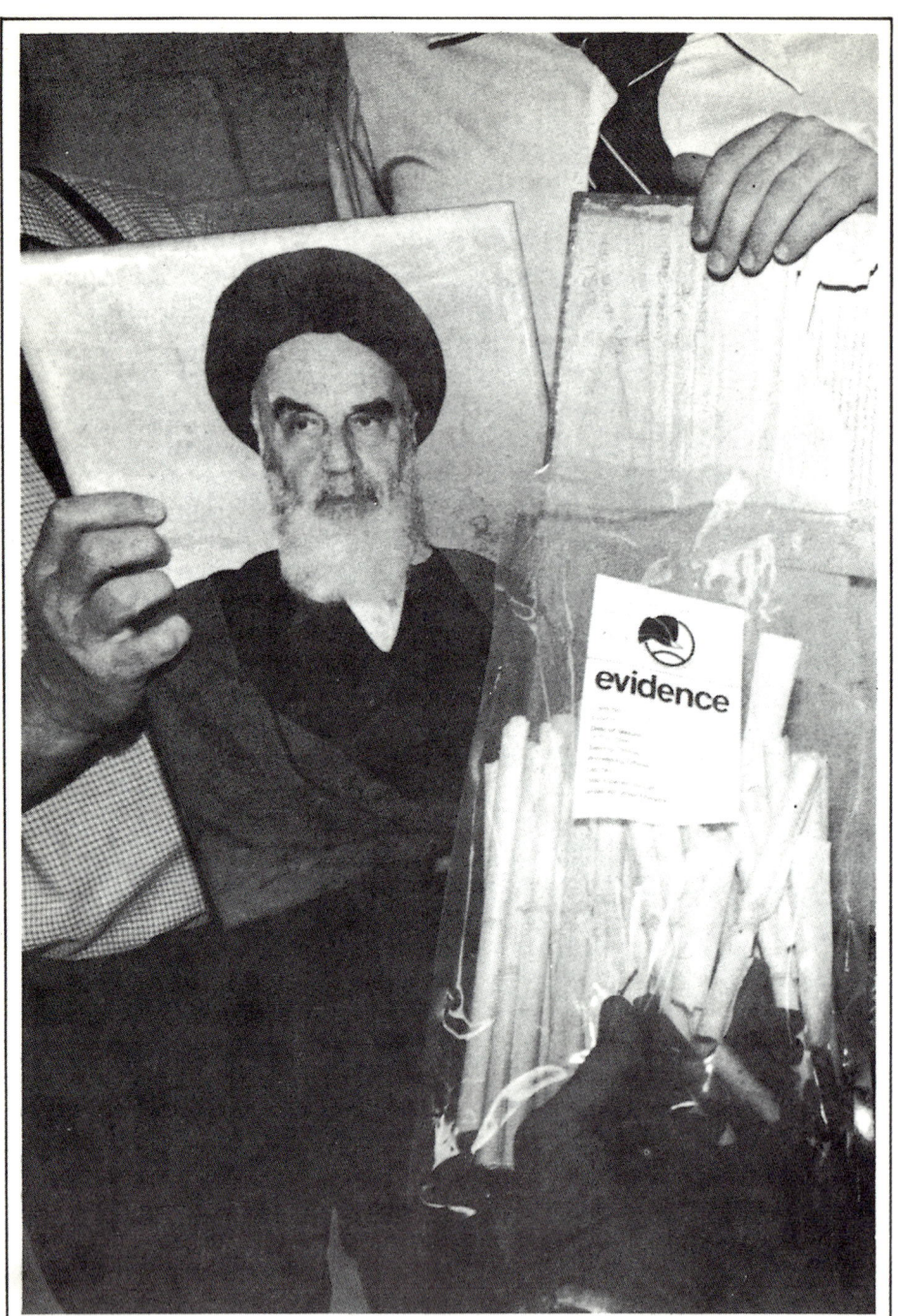

A plastic bag contains opium smuggled into the United States inside pictures of Iran's Ayatollah Ruhollah Khomeini. As little as $500 of raw opium can be converted into $2 million of street heroin on the American market.

CHAPTER 2

HEROIN ADDICTION IN THE MODERN WORLD

Heroin is more expensive than opium. It takes 10 tonnes of opium to produce one tonne of heroin. But opium producers do not have to export much to supply the world market. The entire US addict population uses approximately five tonnes a year, representing only about 2.5% of the annual world production of illegal opium. Fewer than 25 square kilometres of poppy fields can supply the entire US market. The remainder goes to the millions of addicts around the world who are tending to switch from opium to heroin.

Estimating the number of heroin addicts worldwide is difficult for two reasons. First, governments would often prefer to deny or minimize the problem of heroin addiction. Second, addiction is by nature a hidden phenomenon. However, the following facts indicate the extent and character of heroin addiction:

There were an estimated 600,000 to 700,000 addicts in the United States in 1985, most of them living in urban areas. Almost one-third of the US addict population lives in New York City. About 40% are white, 40% are black, and the rest, a growing proportion, are Hispanic and Oriental. Typically, the US addict is a male in his twenties who started using heroin in his late teens. Approximately one-quarter of all heroin addicts are female. Most, but by no means all, addicts are poor. In 1980 an estimated 8,700 people died of heroin overdose in the United States.

In Britain, there were 753 notified opiate addicts in 1964.

By 1985, there were 8,819. Thailand has about as many addicts as the United States, and its largest city, Bangkok, may have 400,000 addicts—almost twice the number estimated to be in New York City.

Italy has 200,000 heroin addicts, who represent a larger percentage of the population than addicts do in the United States.

Pakistan had virtually no heroin addicts in 1979. But by 1985, the country reportedly had more than 150,000 heroin addicts in addition to its opium users.

In recent years, West Germany has reported almost as many deaths attributable to heroin overdose as the United States has.

Several hundred thousand addicts, at a minimum, populate the nations of Malaysia and the Philippines in eastern Asia.

Major cities throughout Mexico and other Latin American countries have serious heroin addiction problems, as do cities in Africa. There is evidence that heroin use is again on the rise in India and even, some observers have said, in China.

Heroin addiction has reportedly been increasing even in the communist bloc nations of Czechoslovakia, Poland and Bulgaria.

Somewhere in Turkey, women sow opium poppy seeds. The legal production of opium for the manufacture of medicines is a carefully controlled agricultural industry in both India and Turkey.

There are countries that have avoided significant problems with heroin, however. One notable example is the Soviet Union, although it has high rates of alcoholism and has recently shown signs of other substance abuse. Even some countries that are nearer to Asian opium sources, such as Japan, South Korea and Taiwan, have escaped large-scale addiction. Political controls or strong cultural taboos and patterns have seemed to effectively prevent opiate use in these nations. But as international travel increases and exposure to other cultures expands, it is unlikely that any nation can remain immune to the spread of drug abuse and addiction.

Worldwide Opium Production and Consumption

Today the legal production of opium for the purpose of manufacturing codeine, morphine and other opium-based medications is a carefully controlled agricultural industry.

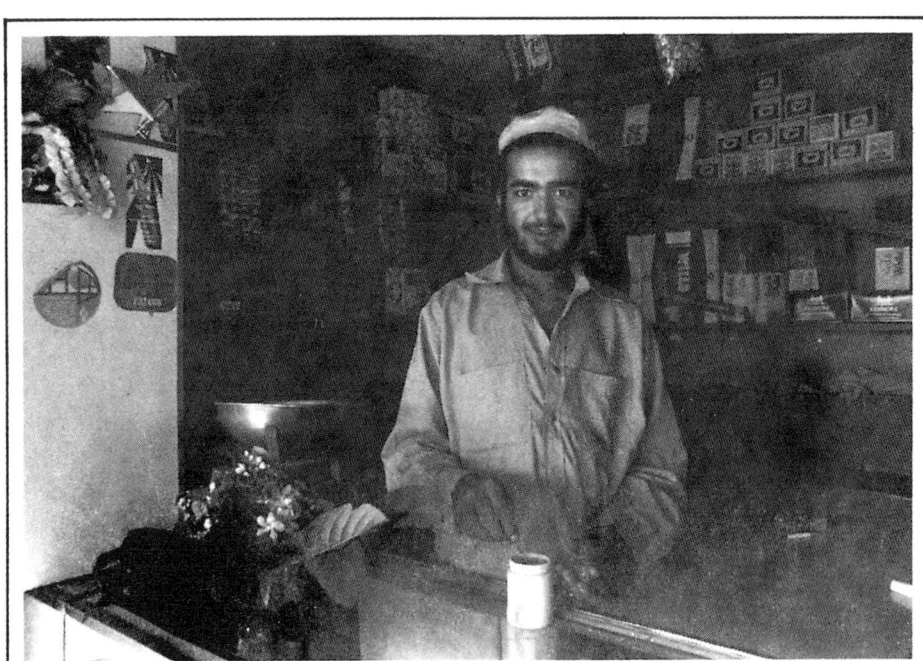

A Pakistani man measures out heroin in his shop. The number of heroin addicts in Pakistan ballooned to 150,000 in 1985, a dramatic increase since 1975, when there were virtually no Pakistani users of the drug.

India is still the leader in this industry, having ended illegal production of opium at the beginning of the 20th century. Currently, Turkey is the second largest grower of legal opium poppies, and smaller quantities are legally grown in a number of other nations, mostly in Europe.

Turkey's illegal suppliers were cut off from their markets when the infamous French Connection smuggling organization, which shipped through the French port of Marseilles, was broken up in the early 1970s. Illegal poppy cultivation is still rampant, however, in the area of southeastern Asia known as the Golden Triangle and in the nations that make up the Golden Crescent in southwestern Asia.

Opium from the Golden Triangle countries—Burma, Thailand, and Laos—became the principal source of the world's heroin after the illegal Turkish trade ended. The war in

Mexican troops leap from a government helicopter in search of illegal poppy and marijuana fields. In 1985, approximately one-third of the heroin smuggled into the United States came from Mexico.

Vietnam also contributed to the development of the black market trade in that region. The war severely disrupted political institutions, government controls and traditional family and community structures. Thousands of US servicemen were comparatively rich, and perhaps naive, new drug customers. Profiteers, always ready to exploit the chaos of war, began to smuggle heroin out of the region. By the mid-1970s, US addicts had found another major source, Mexico. Coarse, brown-coloured heroin was refined from new opium fields in Mexico's mountains and valleys.

Heroin markets grew significantly in the United States and Western Europe until 1978, when severe drought hit the crops of the Golden Triangle. Mexican authorities cooperated with the US and responded quickly to wipe out many of the Mexican opium fields with commercial defoliants. As a

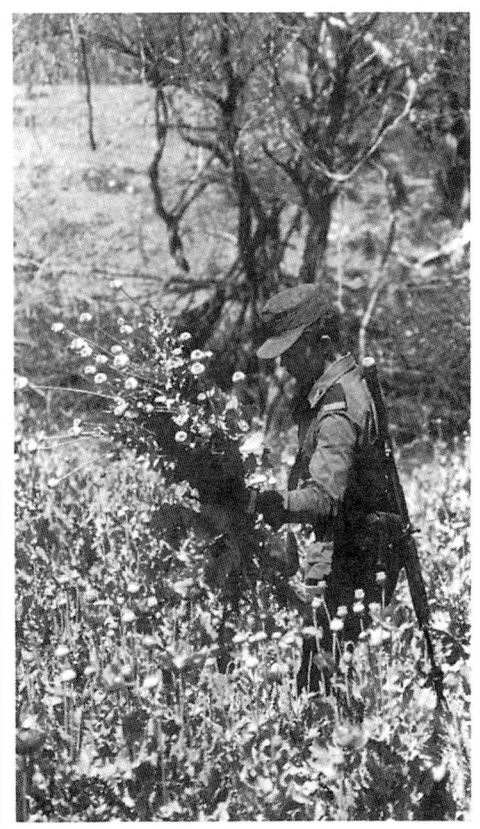

A Mexican soldier in an anti-drug brigade collects illegal poppy plants in Sinaloa. In 1986 United States officials escalated their criticism of the Mexican government for its seeming inability to control drug trafficking.

result, the addict population in the United States fell from an estimated 750,000 to less than 500,000. Soon, however, heroin was being imported from the Golden Crescent, where political turmoil made legal and social controls ineffective. In 1980 the region produced an estimated 1,300 tonnes of raw opium.

The countries of the Golden Triangle and the Golden Crescent continue to undergo powerful social and political stresses, and there is no telling what their impact will be on future opium production. But it is thought that huge opium stockpiles have been hidden away in both regions. In addition, Mexican production has risen again; in 1985 it accounted for approximately one-third of the heroin used in the United States. Barring drastic change, the world will remain amply supplied with heroin for many years.

Why Opium Production Continues

Almost all governments want heroin use ended, and even officials in the nations that supply the drug strongly oppose

An opium grower harvests the spring crop in northwest Pakistan. Although it takes 10 tonnes of opium to produce 1 tonne of heroin, fewer than 10 square miles of poppy fields can provide hundreds of thousands of addicts with enough heroin to last a year.

the opium market. Why are they unable to get rid of the illegal poppy fields?

Huge amounts of opium continue to be cultivated for many reasons. For one thing, opium is a long-established part of many native cultures. Serious political, cultural or ethnic divisions make it extremely difficult for the central governments of supplier nations to maintain control within their own borders. For example, in Iran, government leaders try to exert absolute authority. Yet, discontented minorities, such as the Kurds, bitterly fight the government's control. The Kurdish minority grows, uses and smuggles large quantities of opium out of Iran. The Lao people represent a similar challenge to the authorities in Laos. Profits from opium may even finance wars against the central government itself, as in Afghanistan, where rebel forces smuggle the drug across the mountains to Pakistan in exchange for arms to fight the Soviet-backed regime.

But the major problem seems to be that all the countries where opium poppies are grown are poor. Opium brings growers and labourers more money than almost any other

Workers use a saw-toothed instrument to cut open poppy capsules. Inside the plant is raw opium, which is a milky juice before being dried in the sun and processed into heroin.

crop, sometimes three to five times more, and it is easier to grow. The desperately poor peasants who tend poppy fields are unwilling to give up their profits even though their product causes pain and suffering throughout the world. The local middlemen who organize the growing and smuggling make even more money; sometimes they are government officials who secretly sabotage their own government's efforts to crack down on illegal drug traffic. Even if an illegal operation is stopped, the principal drug traffickers can usually start up new operations elsewhere, enticing growers and labourers with ready cash.

The Black Market

Opium is typically grown in remote areas that are usually separated from government power centres by mountains and deserts. With good weather and the best growing conditions,

Two Afghan rebels share a mount during a raid against Soviet troops in 1980. Rebel forces have smuggled opium across the mountains to Pakistan in exchange for arms to fight the Soviet-backed regime.

each hectare of poppies yields approximately 25 kg of opium. From a local buyer, the villagers may receive in advance the equivalent of a few hundred dollars per hectare, tax-free. Either near the harvest site or in a well-protected location, each 10 kg of opium is refined to 1 kg of morphine, which can be easily transported. The morphine is further refined into 1 kg heroin either at a regional laboratory, which may be only a simple shed or workroom, or at a more distant facility in another country. Each kilogram of the morphine or heroin that has been smuggled out of the remote countryside represents several thousand dollars in market value.

Because of the remote location of the poppy fields, soldiers and police cannot easily locate or get to them to destroy the opium. But growers can smuggle small bags of opium by pack animal or on foot to the refining laboratories. For secrecy and protection, they pay money all along the line of transport. The "fees" usually increase the further along the route the drug goes, and if officials must be bribed, their fees tend to match their authority. For police to track the drug on its way to international transport points means uncovering countless, ever-changing, inconspicuous routes of concealment.

The load of heroin or morphine base soon reaches a port or airfield from which it will leave the country. At this point, each kilogram may be worth $80,000 or more to the principal merchant who has bought it from the regional suppliers, and it represents millions of dollars to Western buyers.

Sometimes private planes or boats carry the drugs on the final leg of the journey across the ocean to the United States. But most often, the heroin is smuggled out on commercial planes or ships. Unless customs officials are tipped off, their chances of intercepting the heroin are very slim. Police would have to tear apart every kind of commercial and personal cargo to find even a few small caches of the drug. Dogs trained to sniff out heroin sometimes help, but heroin is not strongly odorous, and it is usually carefully hidden away in commercial shipments of motor vehicles, TV sets and other manufactured goods. In addition, many smuggling operations pay individuals thousands of dollars to carry heroin on their bodies. Frequently, even body searches are useless because the smugglers often swallow small elastic balloons stuffed with heroin. After passing through customs, they either vomit or excrete the smuggled goods. Of course, if the balloon bursts too soon, the smuggler can die of an overdose.

The arrival of heroin in Western countries requires quick marketing and reaps large profits. The importer is likely to "cut" (dilute) the relatively pure drug with various different substances. It may be milk powder or citric acid, or it may be quinine, or it may be another psychoactive drug like a barbiturate. At every stage of the selling chain the drug may be diluted further. The drug passes from importers to high-level dealers through lower-level dealers until it ends up on the street. Almost all the lower levels of dealers are also addicts who support their own habit in this way. By the time

In the midst of the war between Iran and Iraq, a guerrilla fighter stationed on the border of the two countries shows his wife how to use a foreign-made G-3 rifle. Profits from large quantities of opium smuggled out of Iran may help to finance this war.

the drug is sold at the lowest street level it may be highly impure. Some street drugs in America contain only 5% heroin (sometimes less). Heroin sold in Britain may be less adulterated with about 30-50% heroin at street level. From the raw opium of the producing countries to the streets of Europe and America the drug increases in value to generate huge profits. A kilogram of heroin made from $500-worth of opium may yield $200 million on the streets of New York.

As in the nations that grow the opium, traffickers in the United States pay for secrecy and protection with illegal profits and, consequently often bring corruption to the communities where they operate. An innocent-looking child is sometimes hired at $50 to $100 a day to be a "mule", the person who delivers heroin to addicts, and so protects traffickers from arrest. If arrested, the child is not subject to adult felony charges. Traffickers fortify their warehouses with concrete and steel so that competitors will not steal their heroin and so that, if the police raid them, there will be time to escape or remove the drugs. They hire lookouts with walkie-talkies to alert them to dangers in the neighbourhood, they buy the guns they need to do their own policing, and they pay off authorities who are willing to be bribed. If need be, the top operators have money to buy the best legal defence available. However, it is characteristic of the drug

A Thai woman and her daughter smash open dried opium poppies looking for seeds that will be used to plant next year's crop. The countries of Thailand, Burma, and Laos became the principal source of the world's heroin in the 1970s.

business that the real bosses of the black market do not involve themselves in the actual handling and distributing of the drugs—they make the deals and the money and stay anonymous as far as the street dealers and even more of the middlemen are concerned.

Heroin and Street Crime in the United States

The profits from the heroin trade are ultimately paid for by heroin users and by the innocent people from whom addicts steal in order to support their habit. In some poor cities of southeast Asia, where an injection of heroin costs no more than a glass of beer, the street crime caused by addicts is not as devastating as it is in wealthier Western nations, where

A drug-sniffing dog rips open a package containing illegal substances. In spite of growing federal surveillance efforts, most experts believe that less than 10% of the supply of refined heroin intended for the United States is seized by the authorities.

heroin is far more costly. In the West, robbery, burglary and theft become a career for heroin addicts. Prostitution often becomes the principal livelihood for many female addicts and for some male addicts as well. On both the East and West Coasts, addicts commit an average of three to four felonies apiece every week—more if they are heavy users. Studies show more than one-quarter of all street crime in New York City is committed by heroin users seeking money for drugs. Studies show that more than 20% of all prison inmates are heroin addicts; inmates who are non-addicted heroin users and users of other drugs have committed, on average, less than half as many crimes as heroin addicts; and inmates who do not use any drugs have committed one-seventh as many crimes.

Such studies confirm that with their habit costing up to

Heroin is extremely difficult to detect because it has no strong odour and it is usually concealed in commercial shipments of automobiles, television sets, and other manufactured goods.

$100 a day or more, the hundreds of thousands of US heroin addicts take an enormous toll on property and inflict immeasurable suffering on other people. Since most addicts stay close to their source of heroin, the overwhelming proportion of their victims are the people and businesses in their own neighbourhoods.

Heroin Plus: Addiction and Multidrug Use

When heroin supplies are plentiful and addicts have the cash, they are likely to use only heroin. But even in "good" times, many addicts use other drugs as well. Most addicts become moderate to heavy alcohol-or cannabis-users before they try opiates, and usually they continue to use those drugs even as their heroin use grows. They frequently also use depressant drugs, such as barbiturates, as well as sedatives and stimulants.

Since the late 1970s there has been a rapid increase in the abuse of cocaine. Since the early part of the century there has been a tendency for some addicts to mix heroin and cocaine. The mixture of the stimulant effects of cocaine is said to offset the sedating effects of heroin. The two drugs mixed together into a cocktail are sometimes called a "speedball".

Although there are heroin addicts who start using cocaine as a substitute for scarce opiates, there are reportedly many cocaine-users who try heroin for the first time because they hear that it is very effective at easing the severe physiological letdown that follows heavy cocaine use. For the more than 5 million regular cocaine-users in the United States in 1986, this means that their chances of developing even more drug problems are greater still.

Future Trends

Although there are encouraging trends in some countries, heroin addiction does not appear to be significantly decreasing. On a worldwide basis, the signs are ominous.

An international treaty, *The Single Convention on Narcotic Drugs,* represents the commitment of most governments to coordinate their efforts to break up major smuggling operations and the organizations that run them. Through international cooperation, police and surveillance technologies are becoming more effective, destruction of crops is easier, and more subsidies are being made available to poppy farmers who switch to non-opium crops. United Nations commissions and groups such as the World Health Organization are focusing more of their resources on understanding the problems of addiction and finding ways to help.

Many countries offer school programmes to educate children about the dangers of drug abuse. Anti-drug citizen action groups are proliferating throughout the United States. Some nations, particularly in Asia, sponsor government campaigns to warn citizens of the dangers of narcotics and the severe legal penalties for using them. Many governments under Islamic law, which strictly forbids drug use, are imposing severe penalties, including execution, upon those who are convicted of drug offences. In the United States, another factor may contribute to reducing drug abuse: the percentage of the number of people under 25 is decreasing, a trend that is likely to continue until the end of the century. Most addicts begin using drugs early in life, and people over the age of 25 are statistically much less likely to start using drugs than those under 25.

Heroin addiction in the United States fell off after its peak in the mid-1970s. But use of the drug, which was relatively stable through the early 1980s, rose slightly in the middle of

Pure heroin is cut with dextrose in an illicit drug-processing factory. The substances that dealers use to cut heroin may be anything from quinine to rat poison and can kill a user who injects what he believes is "good stuff."

the decade. One reason is that the price of heroin has gone down, apparently because stockpiled Golden Crescent and Golden Triangle heroin has been put on the market and because heroin now competes with cocaine, which is very expensive. In addition, the use of heroin by middle-class young people and by professional people is increasing.

At the same time, in many countries, the pressure to reduce government spending may delay the upgrading of intelligence, surveillance and enforcement work, without which there is little chance of reducing the supply of heroin. And no matter what penalties the laws impose for drug offences or how many arrests are made, without more courts and prison space the small-time dealers will not be discouraged by the threat of legal consequences. Not the least of the problems is continuing poverty and unemployment, especially in urban areas; wherever large numbers of people live in disillusionment and frustration, the merchants of heroin will find ways to do business.

In fact, social conditions are mainly responsible for the bleak prospects regarding addiction. In most countries,

Despite official denials, narcotics abuse is on the rise in the Soviet Union. The word on the fantasy-sized needle in this cartoon is "narcotics", and the drawing graphically illustrates the menace drug addiction poses to young people all over the world.

including the United States—and especially in developing nations—the populations of cities are swelling at enormous rates. Refugees from the poorer countryside come looking for a better future, only to live in urban slums and shantytowns that breed the conditions of drug addiction. Even in Western Europe, increased immigration and rapidly changing social patterns are accompanied by rising rates of drug abuse, including heroin addiction. Moreover, social change can be a precursor of addiction, and instability and cultural shifts are at work throughout much of Asia and Africa. In contrast to the trend in the United States, in most developing countries the population is getting younger, not older. Just as it was "cool" to use drugs in America in the 1960s and 1970s, many young people in other countries are imitating American styles, and developing American-style drug problems.

A poster warns against heroin, which is dangerous not only to individual users but communities as well – over one-quarter of all street crimes in New York City are committed by heroin addicts seeking drug money.

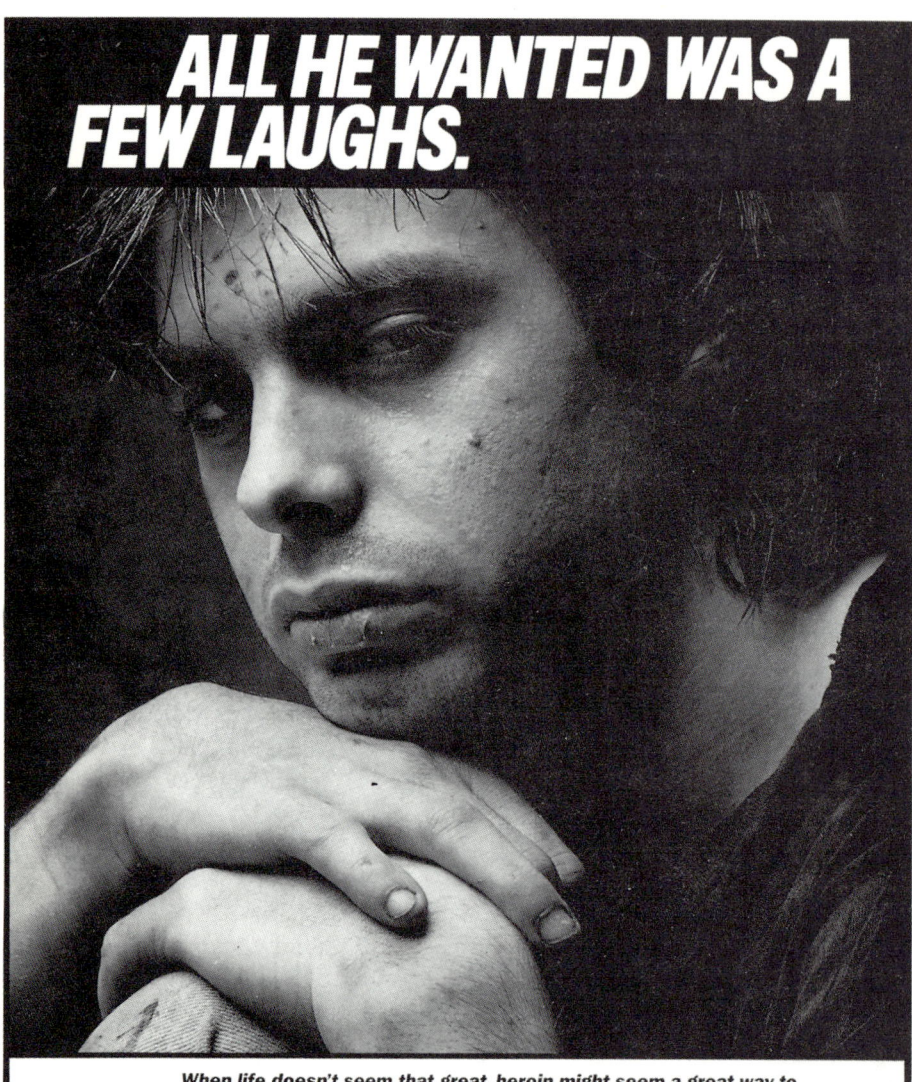

CHAPTER 3

HOW HEROIN AFFECTS ITS USERS

*H*aving looked at what heroin does to whole populations, we now turn to investigating its impact on the individual—upon the body, mind and personality. We will consider both the short-term, or acute, effects and the consequences of continued, or chronic use.

Short-term, Subjective Effects

All opiates behave similarly in the body. In fact, soon after heroin enters the bloodstream, it is converted into morphine by the liver and produces analgesia (pain reduction), just as all opiates do to some degree. But more important to many users is the experience of heroin's intense euphoria.

Heroin's subjective effects—the ones the user feels—are the most powerful effects of any opiate. Injection into the vein brings the most intense and the quickest reaction; it begins within seconds after the injection. For several minutes a pleasant surge, reportedly felt first within the abdomen, spreads throughout the body.

If the dose is heavy enough, however, this rush can bring on unconsciousness or even death. Otherwise, the intense feelings fade within a few minutes and are usually followed by several hours of gradually decreasing sensation, usually accompanied by sleep and lethargy. Feelings of dreaminess may be part of this sleepy period. But, unlike opium, for example, heroin does not cause hallucinations or other distortions of the senses. Regular users often say that heroin makes them feel "peaceful", "painless", "protected", "warm" and "worry-free". But users frequently have difficulties maintaining their concentration and alertness while under the influence. Heroin also produces itching that causes many users to scratch their faces and upper torsos distractedly for hours after an injection.

Heroin can be distinctly unpleasant for many first-time users. Direct injection into a vein often causes the uninitiated to vomit, and other people find the effects disorienting and physically uncomfortable. Unfortunately, this does not always stop experimenters from trying the drug again, and running the risk of addiction. A characteristic of all opiates (and of many other substances, including alcohol) is that the user soon builds up a tolerance to the drug and must steadily increase the amount taken in order to get the same effect.

Acute Physiological Effects

The feelings of euphoria, warmth and protection described above are accompanied by physiological reactions that can be observed and measured by doctors and scientists. Heroin is a depressant, which means that it reduces the key functions of the central nervous system. It slows the pulse and breathing rate, causes a drop in blood pressure, and relaxes the smooth tissues of certain automatically functioning muscles, such as those of the diaphragm and intestines. A person who is high on heroin may therefore exhibit poor coordination, slowed reflexes and slurred speech. The pupils of the eyes are often constricted, the eyes look glazed or watery, and the face may have a feverish flush.

Precisely why heroin produces these and many other changes in the body is not fully known. But during the 1970s scientists and doctors made several important discoveries about the central mechanism underlying the effects of heroin. They found that, once in the bloodstream, opiate molecules attach themselves to certain sites, called receptor sites, on the long nerves, called neurons, that make up part of the brain and central nervous system. The euphoria and analgesia that heroin addicts so crave seem to be switched on when these connections between drug and nerve cell are made.

These findings raised further questions. Above all, scientists wanted to know why opiate molecules fit the neuron receptor sites like keys in a lock. Could it be that the opiates simply resembled other natural substances? The answer proved to be yes, and this discovery has profoundly changed and accelerated not only our understanding of heroin addiction but also much of our understanding about how the brain functions and how chemicals affect our moods and behaviour.

Research teams in the United States and elsewhere began using mice, then rats, and eventually humans in their experiments, and found that the body produces a wide variety of extremely powerful substances that have come to be called endorphins (from Greek words meaning the "morphine inside" us). Responding to signals from the brain, these substances are produced in the pituitary gland and elsewhere, and are constantly released into the bloodstream so that they can attach themselves to the countless millions of receptor sites. Endorphins stimulate electrochemical messages that flow across the neurons and help regulate our responses to stress, pain and all kinds of internal and external events that affect our well-being. Scientists continue to study

Heroin injection can cause serious infections: blood diseases such as hepatitis and collapsed or damaged veins are common among users, and acquired immune deficiency syndrome (AIDS) has become a serious threat to people who share needles.

the very complicated changes involved in the body's lock-and-key mechanisms and continue to find new kinds of locks in the nervous system and new kinds of keys in the body's chemistry. It is now quite clear that heroin and other opiates mimic the effects of the endorphins. Usually, however, opiates enter the body in amounts much greater than the endorphin system was ever designed to receive, and the results are disastrous.

The Dangers of Heroin

Apart from the danger of becoming addicted, a primary risk of using heroin is that of overdosing, particularly if one injects the drug into the vein. Because opiates depress the central nervous system, reducing blood pressure, breathing and muscular functions, a single dose of heroin can cause deep unconsciousness and death. Thousands of users die each year for this reason, and studies show that such deaths may be more common among people who take heroin only occasionally, or who are just beginning to experiment with it, than among heavy regular users who have become tolerant to strong doses. Even if quick medical attention saves the life of an overdose victim, the person can still suffer permanent brain-damage from a lack of oxygen. Less profound unconsciousness under the influence of heroin can and often does result in serious injury if the user collapses suddenly or loses control of a car or some other kind of machinery.

Contrary to earlier beliefs, opiates (unlike alcohol and many other drugs) are no longer considered to be damaging, in and of themselves, to body tissues. But heroin-users rarely consume pure heroin. The adulterants that dealers use to cut heroin or cocaine may be anything from quinine to rat poison and can kill naive users who unwittingly inject contaminated substances.

Injection itself also poses risks. Whether a person injects directly into a vein or just puts the needle under the skin, which is called "skin popping", improper techniques can cause serious infections, including septicaemia (blood poisoning), which may result in the loss of a limb or even in death. After repeated injections in the same place, the veins can collapse or become permanently damaged. A user whose syringe is faulty or who out of carelessness injects some air into the vein may die in as little as a few seconds when a tiny bubble reaches the brain.

Even harder to avoid for many needle-users are diseases that are transmitted by sharing the needles and syringes. Hepatitis, or inflammation of the liver, is one serious disease that has been common among needle-sharers for decades. Similarly, poorly sterilized needles can carry the microorganisms that cause endocarditis, a life-threatening inflammation of the heart lining that is also particularly prevalent among heroin-users. More recently, acquired immune deficiency syndrome, better known as AIDS, has become the most ominous risk of needle-sharing. AIDS is as yet incurable, and it appears to be invariably fatal. And as users contract the

Dr Avram Goldstein (right) was able to isolate an opiate receptor in brain tissue, a discovery that may increase our knowledge of brain chemistry and lead to new ways of understanding and curing addiction.

lethal virus and then, through sexual contact with others, transmit it to the non-addict community, their drug habits bring death to the population at large.

The dangers of using heroin exists even for occasional or new users. But the dangers increase the more a person uses the drug.

Dependence and Addiction

The words "dependence" and "addiction" are commonly used today to describe a broad range of relationships between an individual and a substance or activity. For example, people described as "workaholics" are considered to be to some degree addicted to work. Similarly, many individuals say that they are addicted to chocolate. When referring to drug abuse, however, we assign each word a distinctly different meaning.

When opiates and several other classes of drugs (such as sedatives, depressants and stimulants) are used regularly and heavily, they cause physiological changes to such an extent that the body will undergo predictable distress should use of the drug be abruptly stopped. This condition is called dependence.

As dependence increases, so does an individual's tolerance. It is important to understand that one becomes tolerant to both toxic and euphoric effects. This means that a heroin dose that barely gives a heavy user any pleasure could be fatal to someone who has less experience with the drug.

The suffering that a dependent person goes through upon abruptly ceasing drug use is called "withdrawal". With opiates, the withdrawal syndrome resembles a case of flu. Chills and gooseflesh, runny nose, aching limbs, abdominal cramps, vomiting and diarrhoea are all common symptoms. Though it can be very uncomfortable, withdrawal is not a life-threatening condition. But the drive to avoid "dope sickness" becomes a powerful force that sustains opiate use. And as every experienced heroin addict knows, a shot of heroin brings immediate, though temporary, relief when withdrawal is underway.

The withdrawal syndrome typically begins within 8 to 12 hours following a dependent person's last dose of heroin. Usually the symptoms peak within a day or two and ease considerably within 3 to 5 days, but insomnia and irritability may persist for weeks. The severity of withdrawal varies with the amount, frequency and duration of opiate use during the episode of dependence. More intense and sustained symptoms follow heavier, more chronic use. Psychological factors also play a significant role. Social support and one's physical environment during withdrawal, one's desire for abstinence, the availability of alternative opiates, and other factors affect the intensity of the withdrawal. A heroin-dependent person who is in jail and who still wants heroin may feel more sick than a dependent user who enters a caring and drug-free environment with a strong motivation to get off the drug.

A 24-year-old heroin addict serves a prison term for burglary. The urgent need to get high has caused many opiate users to commit increasingly desperate acts of theft and violence.

Studies with opiate-dependent rats reveal that simply being in an environment where the animal has previously undergone repeated withdrawal episodes—a special cage, for instance—can cause withdrawal symptoms to occur again even when the animal is no longer dependent.

In any event, the withdrawal syndrome flares up and subsides relatively quickly, and normal physiological functioning usually returns in a few weeks or less. The person's tolerance to opiates will also drop off sharply. This means that if a person takes opiates soon after withdrawal, the effect from a given dose will be stronger than it was during

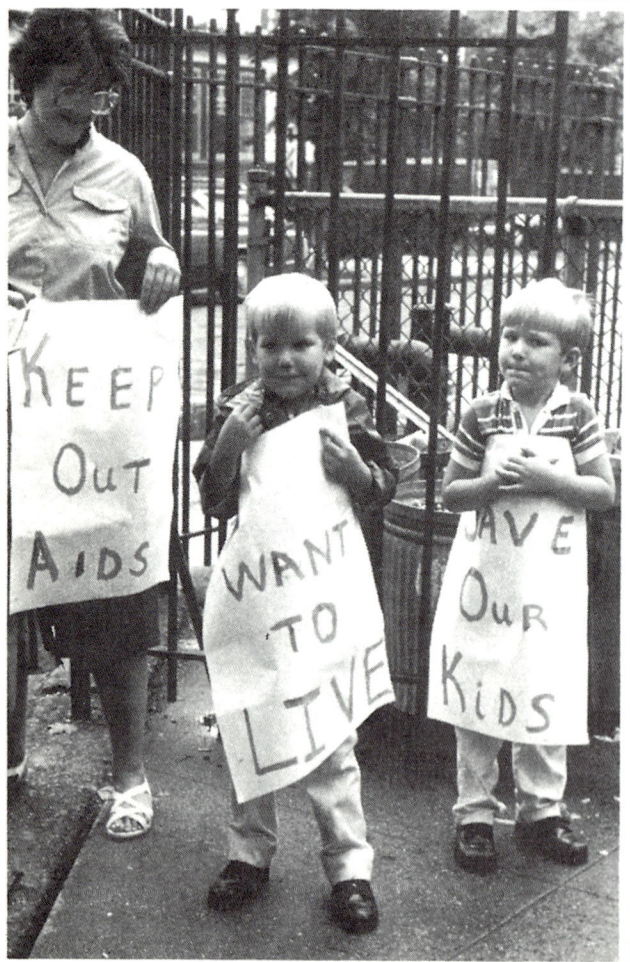

Many young children have contracted the incurable and deadly disease AIDS from transfusions of blood contaminated with the virus. Heroin addicts are especially vulnerable to this illness and are partly responsible for introducing AIDS into the blood supply.

dependence. Overdoses are especially common in such cases.

During a career of heroin use, a person may undergo repeated episodes of full or partial withdrawal. One method of withdrawal is to end all drug use abruptly ("going cold turkey") and suffer acute withdrawal. A second method is to be weaned from dependence with gradually decreasing doses of opiates so that the suffering is minimized. No matter how withdrawal is accomplished, a person is no longer dependent once he or she is opiate-free and has recovered from the effects of withdrawal.

Once dependence has ended, is a person cured? The withdrawal pains may have passed, but a more insidious drive—addiction—usually persists. As used here "addiction" means the urge, or craving, to use opiates that can occur repeatedly long after physical dependence has ended. These urges are most often related to opiate use in the past. For example, a former user may suddenly want to get high upon seeing an old friend with whom he or she formerly used heroin. Holding large sums of cash, feeling very stressful and lonely and, above all, having opiates easily available can also trigger strong cravings. Psychologists call this a conditioned response. Just as the dogs in the famous experiment by the Russian scientist Ivan Pavlov salivated for food, so addicts crave opiates when any of their psychological or environmental "bells" ring.

If physical dependence can be ended relatively simply, what about addiction? Addiction stems from unconscious conditioning, and addicts may truly not recognize that they are under the power of the drug and the things that trigger its use. "Don't worry", says the addict, "I know what I'm doing". In reality, with each new occasion of drug-craving and drug-taking, the compulsion becomes more deeply rooted. However, addiction can be greatly reduced and controlled by reversing the conditioning process. This requires abstinence, usually for a year or more, while the person adopts drug-free responses to drug-craving. We will discuss this process in greater detail in a later chapter. But one vital point needs to be made here: even "recovered" addicts may still feel a desire for opiates. More significantly, if a person uses opiates, even after a long period of abstinence, the craving response can be strengthened quickly, and the individual will experience a rapid return of high tolerance if regular drug use resumes. So, in attempting even a limited use of opiates, recovering addicts court disaster. Dependence and addiction can return at an ever-accelerating rate.

The Impact of Chronic Heroin Use on Personality and Lifestyle

The details vary from case to case, but the downward course of a heroin addict's life is all too familiar and predictable. As drug procurement and use start to become more frequent, secretiveness is usually the first change in behaviour that the user's family and friends notice. The user's time will be spent increasingly on drugs, either with other drug-users or alone. Friends, family and activities that were once important will be ignored. Disturbed sleeping habits may develop. Psychological stresses will grow as the user experiences and tries to rationalize and defend this new behaviour. As tolerance to the drug builds, anger and depression may increasingly accompany the chronic user's high, even as the drug's

An opium addict in the first stages of withdrawal, one of the symptoms of which is dramatic chills – although the temperature is over 90°F, this man is huddled under blankets for extra warmth.

euphoric effects grow milder and briefer. Close friends and family often become the targets of hostility or used as a source of money for drugs. Most addicts borrow heavily and use everyone they know to get cash.

Indeed, as addiction continues, those with whom the addict sustains relationships will usually become tools (consciously or unconsciously) of the addiction. Real intimacy between the user and anyone else will be all but impossible. For example, addicts' sexual relations are virtually non-existent during episodes of heavy dependence. Chronic, heavy opiate use impairs sexual functioning and reduces interest in sex. The only exception is prostitution, which addicts often engage in to get drug money.

Although some heroin addicts can manage to keep their jobs, usually the urgent need to obtain drugs and get high rules out any kind of steady work or study schedule. Absenteeism, grossly impaired performance, or theft from the workplace cost most addicts their jobs, usually resulting in even more desperate behaviour: more drug use, more theft, more alienation and dishonesty.

Personal hygiene will suffer as the downward trend intensifies. Dietary needs will be ignored. Constipation can be chronic because opiates relax the smooth muscle tissue of the bowels. Medical treatments become for the addict merely a means of getting opiates. The long-term addict is usually reduced to a lifestyle that is entirely dominated by the drive to experience an opiate high. Cheap lodgings become home, and going to "shooting galleries" (rooms or abandoned buildings where groups of addicts meet to inject their heroin) becomes the main social activity of most addicts. Theft and increasingly desperate acts of violence are the norm within this drug culture. In the end, the addict becomes little more than a tool and a vessel, obtaining and taking as much heroin and other opiates as possible.

In the meantime, the addict either prevents or distorts the day-to-day experiences that help develop maturity and stamina. This is why many former users, even after achieving abstinence and working hard to undo all the damage of their drug habit, find everyday life extremely difficult and suffer from deep self-contempt and hopelessness. Many long-term users express a desire to end it all with an overdose; perhaps many fatal injections are indeed deliberate.

Three Portraits

The following individuals are fictitious, but they are composites drawn from real life that accurately portray the lifestyles and personalities so common among the users of heroin.

James

Now in his late twenties, James had been an obedient and quiet child. He and several siblings grew up in a poor neighbourhood and learned to avoid making trouble for their mother and to stay out of the way of their alcoholic, abusive father. Even before his teens, James turned to the streets for excitement. There, like his older brother and sisters, he could

Approximately one kilogram of heroin smuggled through Heathrow, in a brandy bottle. Rates of heroin use are high in both rapidly changing traditional cultures and in modern urban neighbourhoods.

assert his independence and be seen as capable by his peers. His use of alcohol and cannabis increased quickly once he dropped out of school, and he began to commit petty crimes. By his 14th year, James was smoking heroin regularly and soon began using it intravenously.

Since then, James has known a life mainly centred on heroin. He has been in and out of the courts, prison and, with hardly more enthusiasm, treatment programmes. For James, treatment has been a chance to lower his tolerance in order

Studies show that the poorer urban areas, typified by overcrowded, squalid conditions, have a high number of heroin addicts and dealers.

to get an easier high, and going to jail is just a part of the lifestyle that he and many of his friends accept and share. Apart from his criminal abilities, James has developed few skills. Indeed, the straight life appears to him to be a more oppressive and pointless existence than the one he has. He would like to be a source of pride to the mother he loves so much and a good role model for the children he has fathered by various women, but he sees no way to achieve conventional success. He believes he will die from an overdose or from some violent consequence of his lifestyle, and he accepts drug addiction as his destiny.

Sue

Sue comes from a conservative middle-class family, and before she entered college—where, like many of her classmates, she started to smoke cannabis and drink—she never took drugs. She was eager to excel as an art student and had professional ambitions. To help her study when she was tired or had drunk too much, she sometimes used the amphetamine pills a doctor had prescribed for weight control. The pills made her feel creative and bright even when she drank. When she started going out with a pharmacy student who had access to various opiates, Sue decided she liked their effects even more. She managed to graduate from college, but not before beginning to inject morphine supplied by her boyfriend and, when she could get it, heroin. After she graduated from college, she socialized primarily with other drug-users and she usually had one boyfriend or another who could get heroin for her.

Sue has now been addicted to heroin and other strong opiates such as morphine for close on 20 years. She has experienced some periods of abstinence from these hard drugs, replacing them with alcohol or sedatives, but she has rarely been entirely drug-free for more than a few days at a time. She has had numerous medical problems, and from her many visits to doctors and hospitals she has learned to manipulate a network of medical professionals to get prescriptions for opiates. Her income has come mainly from unemployment benefit, low-level jobs in art galleries, and prostitution when she is desperate. She also shoplifts regularly. Although she has been arrested several times, she has never been put in jail.

Sue still cannot easily acknowledge her addiction. She prefers to see herself as a professional whose career has been afflicted with bad luck, illness and the failure of professional contacts and old friends to help out. But, as she enters her forties, it is harder for her to deny that drugs have blighted her life. In recent years, she has made efforts to find legitimate work and stay drug-free, but then she gets depressed or ill and relapses. Usually the drugs available to her through her friends tempt her to go back to the drug habit. Most of the people she knew before her life was

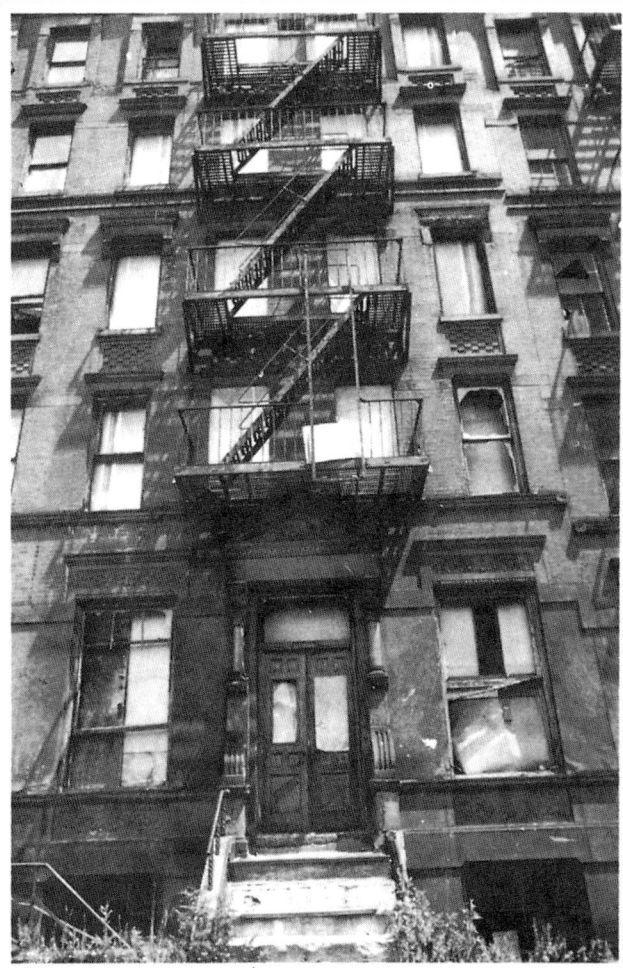

"Shooting galleries" are often flats or abandoned buildings where groups of addicts converge to prepare and inject their heroin, a ritual that becomes the dominant social activity for most addicts.

completely taken over by drug-use no longer welcome her, and her immediate family has rejected her outright.

Mike

Mike was always somewhat mischievous but never got into serious trouble until his early twenties, when he and his girlfriend started taking the opiate oxycodone which some friends gave out at parties. They both enjoyed the effects but she soon stopped taking the pills after she almost caused a fatal car accident while she was high. Mike continued using oxycodone and felt that it actually helped him deal more confidently with clients at work. His girlfriend disapproved. He told her he had stopped, but secretly continued to buy the drug and use it more and more. Although Mike had heard that all opiates were addicting, he believed that as long as oxycodone helped him and he did not use heroin, he was in no danger. However, when he was unable to get the drug, he felt sick and frequently missed work. He eventually relaxed his scruples about heroin, and began using this street drug in addition to oxycodone. His relationship with his girlfriend suffered, too, even though they both avoided the subject of drugs.

About six months after he started taking oxycodone, Mike was caught stealing from petty cash at work and was fired. His parents took him in, believing that he had a "drink problem", as Mike put it. They also gave him money to pay off his debts. But he was using drugs more than ever, selling his personal possessions (and even some of his girlfriend's) to buy heroin from his friends. Finally, a few days after Mike's mother discovered some jewellery missing, she found him unconscious in the bathroom with a syringe still in his arm. Mike spent a night in the hospital and then entered a residential treatment centre.

He worked hard to restore himself to health and to understand what drugs had done to him. When he was discharged, his family and his girlfriend welcomed him back with love and support. His employer even rehired him. Soon, he and his girlfriend got married and everyone tried to forget the past.

Despite some strong cravings, Mike stayed drug-free for nearly a year. Then a dentist prescribed oxycodone to ease the pain for some dental work. Mike took more than the recommended dose because he felt it was inadequate. When he ran out of medication, he called some old friends who supplied him with a lot more. On and off for a month, Mike struggled against renewed urges to get high, occasionally giving in and snorting some heroin. No one at work or at home wanted to confront him about the changes in behaviour and mood that they observed. But it was not too long before a full relapse was obvious to everyone; Mike had returned to daily intravenous use of heroin and, increasingly, cocaine. When new thefts were discovered at work, Mike's employer had him arrested "for his own good". Mike re-entered treatment knowing he had a choice between treatment and jail.

An officer inspects drug-manufacturing equipment after a raid. The many tonnes of heroin that are smuggled into Western countries every year yield enormous amounts of wealth, in profits, for the bosses of the black market.

HOW MUCH CAN HEROIN COST YOU?

It can cost you your looks.

It can cost you your family.

It can cost you your health.

It can cost you your possessions.

It can cost you your mates.

It's not long before heroin costs you far more than just money. So even if a friend offers you some for nothing, tell them the cost is too high.

HEROIN SCREWS YOU UP.

CHAPTER 4

THEORIES OF HEROIN ADDICTION

*F*or many years, heroin addiction has not only been the classic form of drug addiction in the mind of the public, but also the principal focus of professionals who study non-alcoholic drug addiction in general. Because it is a disorder that affects so many aspects of life, researchers in psychology, sociology, physiology and various fields of medicine have investigated heroin's impact on human well-being. There is as yet no one theory of addiction that all the researchers agree on, but this chapter reviews some of the major ideas that are being explored. It also ties some of these ideas together so that we can understand in a commonsense way how and why people become heroin addicts.

Is Heroin Addiction a Disease?

For centuries, drug addicts were commonly regarded as the victims of their own wilful immorality. Even after it became known that chronic use of opiates produces physical dependence, people continued to believe that to develop dependence by over-using opiates and, worse, to use them again after detoxification indicated a flawed character and/or low intelligence.

Sharing the insights of Islamic physicians of a thousand years earlier, the British became the first to institutionalize another view. They felt that addiction was better understood as a kind of disease. And today, almost all authorities on addiction agree with this idea. But what does it mean to say that addiction is a disease? Does it mean that, like a cancer, addiction literally has a life of its own that can overpower even the most moral and responsible person? Or that something goes haywire in a person's brain and the only thing a person can do about it is take heroin? The answer is not that simple.

"Disease" usually means an abnormal condition in a living organism that can be recognized by a set of signs, or symptoms, that follow a standard course and that represent a threat to the well-being and full functioning of the organism. Heroin addiction does seem to fit this general description. The confusion and controversy over calling addiction a disease have to do primarily with how much conscious control a person has over beginning and ending drug use. Most diseases begin without our being aware of it. Invisible viruses or poisons in the environment may invade the body, or genes that were defective from birth may slowly begin to trigger serious problems after years of inactivity. In contrast, drug addiction would seem to begin only if a person chooses to take an addicting drug. But if drug-taking is, in a sense, self-

Billie Holiday, a famous jazz and blues singer in the 1930s and 1940s, also made headlines for repeated narcotics arrests. Her struggle with a heroin dependency brought national attention to the complex problem of drug anticipation.

inflicted, addiction itself is not; it develops not at the direction of one's will, but as the replacement of will. And, as we will discuss later, some people may suffer from problems that make them prone to drug use and addiction. However, for people who understand the danger of drugs and are careful to avoid the temptations, addiction is relatively preventable. Similarly, increased knowledge and responsible action make many diseases—such as heart disease, certain cancers, or tooth decay—more preventable. So the disease concept is also applicable to a definition of addiction; a person can rarely overcome addiction simply by choosing to be done with it, any more than a person can choose to get over heart disease.

But there is one aspect of drug addiction that distinguishes it from other diseases. Taking drugs, especially heroin, can be very pleasurable. So how can we say that heroin addicts have a disease when their problems seem to have so much to do with experiencing euphoria? There is a possible explanation: one feature of heroin addiction is a drive for chemically

Babies born to narcotic-dependent mothers can experience withdrawal symptoms such as rigidity and tremors. Here, a doctor cradles an infant recovering from heroin withdrawal as the child's mother, a former addict, looks on.

induced physical satisfaction so strong that the addict's whole life becomes unmanageable.

It should be remembered that the disease concept is not a theory of addiction, but rather a way of thinking about the issue and forming questions that theorists then try to answer—questions about why people begin to abuse drugs such as heroin, how physical dependence develops, and why people who have "kicked" and "cleaned up" relapse so often, even though they know the dangers and have committed themselves to abstinence.

Conditioning

We know that opiates can be strong reinforcers, meaning that they reward the user's central nervous system with euphoric feelings and can dramatically relieve the distress of withdrawal. The more a person uses heroin and experiences these short-term rewards, the more conditioned the person is likely to become to the drug's effects. The reinforcement does not have to be powerful each time the person uses the drug. So even if addicts with high tolerance get a major reward only when they inject an especially large dose, that can be enough to keep the conditioning going strong.

Scientists often propose conditioning as the central dynamic of heroin addiction. Experiments with laboratory animals such as rats and monkeys, which have nervous systems like ours, have proved conclusively the powerful reinforcing properties of morphine and heroin. But human responses are complicated by many other factors, such as personality and social environment. In addition, no one knows exactly why reinforcement operates in the nervous system of either animals or humans. So, while conditioning probably plays an essential role in heroin addiction, we need to look elsewhere to see how it fits into the wider picture.

Personality Factors

Whereas many people still characterize heroin addicts as immoral, psychiatrists try to understand what lies behind their deviant attitudes and behaviour. For example, recent studies have demonstrated that heroin addicts have typically been more deviant in their youth than other people, but we cannot say why. In some of the earlier studies of addicts who were evaluated in prisons or while they were actively engaged in their addict lifestyles, heroin-users frequently demonstrated the kinds of thinking and behaviour that psychiatrists call psychopathic. A psychopath is considered to be lacking the instincts that are essential for forming caring human relationships and to be resistant to the lessons of experience. Psychopaths are manipulative and devious, and they are always apt to blame others for the problems their own behaviour causes. The psychological concept of the addict as psychopath thus fits the old stereotype of the "bad" addict.

As a result, the psychiatrists who began modern testing and evaluation of addicts at the Addiction Research Centre in Lexington, Kentucky, during the 1930s and 1940s expected to learn more about the criminal mind. But both the Lexington studies and extensive psychosocial research conducted since that time failed to define a particular personality profile that characterized most addicts or that suggested something about a common tendency. Instead, the researchers encountered a great range of personality features. Most

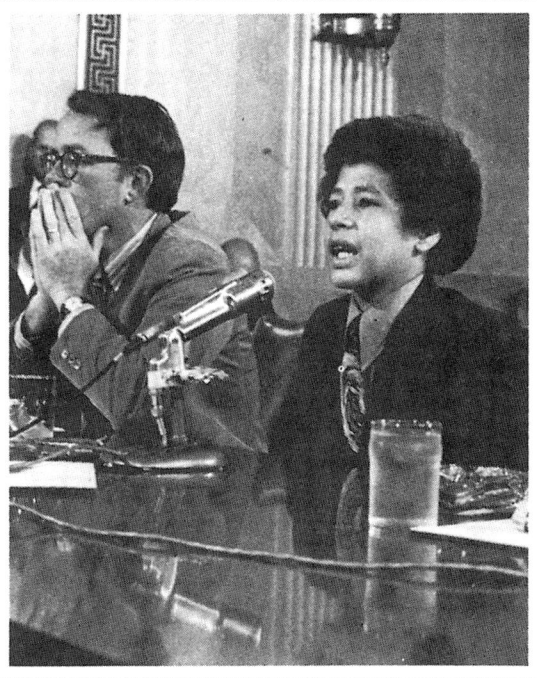

"It is easier to get heroin than to get liquor," commented this teenage ex-addict from Queens, New York, who spoke to the Senate Government Operations subcommittee about his experience with drugs.

experts now think that the earlier findings were based on observation of the effects of addiction and addicted lifestyles, and on the possibility that the more sociopathic addicts were the ones most likely to be imprisoned and written about. Difficulties in assessing the true personalities of heavy drug-users continue because it is quite difficult to know whether an addict's thoughts, feelings and behaviour are the result of the addiction experience or whether they preceded and contributed to the addiction.

Since the 1960s, new characterizations of the addict have begun to replace the sociopathic one. Various psychological needs have been cited by theorists as factors that drive some people to use drugs—and in particular to use heroin. Today, the term "addictive personality" is used to describe a person with these overpowering needs. Like the disease concept, the addictive personality concept is only a way of thinking about the issue and not a theory or a set of facts. The term is probably used most consistently to refer to people who, for one reason or another, are thought to have an obsession with drugs, food, dependent relationships or certain activities such as gambling or even shopping, and who can never really end their addiction but can only switch from one abnormal attachment to another.

Most authorities in the field of addiction think that a better way to understand why people become addicted is to consider the proneness (the vulnerability or tendency toward addiction) that a person might have. The following

Some psychological studies suggest that low self-esteem, which is one effect of alcoholism, is often present in potential heroin addicts as well.

are a few of the major personality characteristics that are believed to make an individual prone to drug abuse.

Personality and Addiction

One psychological condition widely seen in heroin addicts is low self-esteem—which includes the belief that one is a failure or incompetent, related feelings of hopelessness, and sometimes general psychological depression. Some psychologists have said that heroin addicts suffer from a disorder named hypophoria, a kind of depression that is specifically related to low self-esteem. "Why shouldn't I take drugs if they make me feel good? I'm a loser anyway" is the presumed attitude of this kind of person.

Another common observation is that addicts often seem to be strangely dependent on one family member or on the family as a whole for emotional support and acceptance, or develop an unusual attachment to a spouse or lover. Some theorists interpret this behaviour as signalling problems with what is called individuation—the maturation process of establishing one's own sense of identity and capacities for independent choice and actions. Since many addicts begin using drugs in adolescence, one possibility is that a very troubled individuation process made them prone to using drugs to get immediate feelings of warmth and security. Another possibility is that addiction in adolescence causes users to get stuck in immature stages of individuation.

Psychiatrists who have paid close attention to their addicted patients' unconscious psychological processes suggest that addicts suffer from repressed or buried feelings, such as grief or anger, that they feel are too powerful to let out. Sometimes the cause of the anger is thought to be the absence of sufficient parental love in childhood. Sometimes it is associated with the loss or death of a close family member or other important person. Increasingly, physical and sexual abuse are being considered as possible causes for repressed anger or sadness. Sociologists say that oppressive living conditions contribute to feelings of rage or abandonment that the addicts finds too powerful to acknowledge consciously and cope with. Because heroin initially suppresses mental pain and angry feelings, its use is sometimes regarded by psychiatrists as a form of self-medication for unconscious emotional disturbances.

Still another theory about unconscious reasons for using drugs is put forth by therapists who observe families as social systems. They believe that the addict is often unconsciously acting out the whole family's psychological problems. This theory also points to the role of other family members who, also unconsciously, may even be getting satisfaction from the addiction. A relatively simple example of the family-system theory might be that of an abusive husband, his wife and their addicted son. The son's addiction serves as an excuse for the parents to avoid their own problems, punishes the father, numbs the son to his anger, and gives the mother a person to whom she can devote special care and from whom she can get loving gratitude. The family-system theory says that, like the addict, all the other family members tend to get locked into positions and attitudes that keep the drug-use going because that is easier than focusing on their real problems.

Several of the above theories can be put under the general heading of adaptive theories about heroin use. They assert that psychological conditions may make people prone to using heroin in order to adapt to difficult conditions that they do not have the strength to handle unaided but are not actually trying to escape from. Many addicts confirm that when they began to use heroin they found that it gave them the feelings of security and confidence they lacked; that the drug made them feel better able to handle inner conflict personal relationships, and sexual intimacy; and that it generally made them feel "more together".

There is, however, a popular theory that suggests a very different reason for heroin use. The theory proposes that, because of their low self-esteem, some people become addicted in order to punish themselves or slowly commit suicide. After years of addiction, it is not uncommon for heroin addicts to support this theory. They may at times express a great deal of self-hatred and are quite willing to believe that their continued injection of heroin, near overdoses and close brushes with death and disaster must relate to self-destructive desires. However, few addicts begin their drug careers conscious of any "death wish" or pursuit of pain, and therefore if these feelings are at work, they probably begin unconsciously and develop well into the addictive experience.

THEORIES OF HEROIN ADDICTION

In contrast to either the adaptive or self-destruction explanations, another theory of addiction makes the case that because psychological and ego development have been impaired, some people have an abnormally low ability to delay gratification. Thus, a person may have strong needs for pleasure that cannot be met through the conventional means of applying oneself to a sustained task. Such a person may be prone to finding the very quick and intense effects of drugs — however spurious and destructive they may be in the long run — all too appealing.

A theme that runs through many theories about the addict's personality is that drug-users are often responding to feelings of emptiness and futility. Unlike depression or low self-esteem, this psychological state is said to come not from the person's own problems but from a perception that there is nothing worth striving for and that life in general is meaningless. Psychologists sometimes call this the existential factor because it relates to basic questions about the purpose of existence. The pursuit of dangers and thrills that characterizes the lives of some drug-users may be their way of getting in touch with their own life force, and drugs may add to the excitement. For others who suffer from existential emptiness, heroin may seem to numb the pain of feeling that life is pointless.

Many people—particularly members of organizations such as Alcoholics Anonymous (AA) and its companion organization Narcotics Anonymous (NA)—interpret any psychological suffering that leads to the use of heroin as an escape or an adaptive "crutch", to be a sign of spiritual impairment. Spirituality in this case refers to feeling connected with an ultimate and nourishing reality, whether it is God or some other source of meaning and strength. These spiritual doctrines about addiction state that if a person lacks faith and does not live as that faith prescribes, the pain and emptiness of life can make drugs dangerously seductive; moreover, if a person does become addicted, then only faith in a "higher power" (the term used by AA and NA) can free the person from that slavery.

Social Factors

No individual, not even the profoundly isolated heroin addict, lacks a social setting and a social history. Everything we feel and do occurs in the context of our relationships with other people. The following ideas about social influences are

It is hard to equate this tribeswoman from Thailand with the desolation of an addict, but, by selling opium pods she is part of the influential drug-trafficking personnel.

among those that figure most prominently in theories of heroin addiction.

Availability

Making heroin available is surely the most obvious part that other people can play in the development of any individual's addiction; research shows that when drug supplies increase, the rate of new addictions usually does, too. But the availability of heroin alone is not enough to get a person started. Consider the historical cases of India and Turkey, where top-grade opium was grown in abundance for years. Those societies never had the addiction problems of the nations they supplied. And within a given society (the United States for example), some population groups have had much higher addiction rates than others, even though opiates were widely available to all groups. If, instead of focusing on availability, we focus on addiction-prone personalities, we still must ask why there are so many drug problems in certain population groups. There is no evidence that proneness to opiate addiction has to do with factors such as racial or ethnic differences, the physical environment, or the food eaten in certain cultures.

Peer Pressure

Most researchers believe that next to availability, the key social factor that determines whether a person will use the drugs is the influence of his or her peers. Indeed, drug availability and interactions with one's friends often go literally hand-in-hand; users usually get their first drugs from their friends. Most heroin-users begin using drugs earlier than abusers of other hard drugs, although they rarely start with heroin. Cigarettes, alcohol and cannabis (typically in that order) precede heroin, and social research demonstrates that adolescent peers who use these substances are almost always part of the young user's circle of friends.

Of course, not everyone follows the example of others, and often a young person will have several distinct peer groups with which to associate. Therefore social theorists, like most personality theorists, view peer influence as a contributor to a propensity for using drugs, not as a direct cause.

Social Learning

The apparent power of peer influence suggests to many social psychologists that addiction may have a social learning component. "Social learning" refers rather generally to how we acquire skills and attitudes and take on certain roles as a result of belonging to a social system where such behaviour is modelled in everyday life by our peers. It is said that through social learning, less experienced peers are not just offered heroin or encouraged to use it, but are actually *taught* to use it and appreciate it. And, through the example and approval of more experienced peer users, they learn the lifestyle of addiction.

Slightly older young people, whose tough, daring and "cool" behaviour allows them to dominate their peer group, are the stereotype of the role model who sets the standard of drug use. But a role model can be anyone a person imitates for any reason. Research reveals that heroin addicts and abusers of other drugs are more apt than non-users to have family members who abuse alcohol or other drugs. Some psychologists suggest that this pattern results in social learning of drug abuse within families; other scientists claim that it is evidence of genetic factors that run in certain families, making them prone to addiction.

Social controls

A community's social controls also have a major effect on drug use. This concept has as much to do with the average citizen's response to drug abuse as it does with the legal system. Social controls are said to be strong when, for example, families in a given neighbourhood share similar rules for their children, and neighbours are watchful of other families' children and quick to report to the parents any violation of those rules. Traditional cultures, like India's, frequently have strong social controls that make it very difficult for someone to violate standards of behaviour without being exposed and quickly reprimanded by other members of the society. Thus, it is argued, even though opium was grown in India and was for a while aggressively marketed there opiate use was kept within certain limits by local customs.

Communities and cultures in transition usually suffer a weakening of social controls. When new populations move in, when economic conditions change significantly, or when new products or technology begin to change daily life, community standards may become confused. The expression of community approval or disapproval may carry less weight and more deviance from the old standards may appear. Sociologists point to the high rates of heroin use both in rapidly changing traditional cultures and in modern urban neighbourhoods, where change is constant, as evidence that where social controls are weak, addiction tends to spread.

Of course, living amid rapid change can also be personally stressful; so is living where crime and poverty are widespread. Continual personal stress, whatever the cause, is one of the most widely accepted factors that make a person prone to drug abuse. And where frightening street crime, high unemployment, or generally unhealthy living conditions are features of everyday life, personality disorders of all sorts—including drug abuse—have a much higher than average incidence.

Setting

One of the most significant modern studies of heroin addiction focused on American servicemen in Vietnam, many of whom became addicted to smoking or injecting the heroin that was cheap and plentiful throughout Southeast Asia during the war. Military treatment programmes had very little success in preventing relapses among those patients who returned to active duty in Vietnam. But only about 5% of the soldiers who became addicted there continued to be chronic heroin-users once they returned to the United States. A leading interpretation of this remarkable finding is that aspects of a particular setting can go a long way in determining how a person in that setting relates to drugs. In the case of the American servicemen, the stress of the battle, the availability of heroin, the attitudes and behaviour of peers, and the lack of effective social controls upon American military personnel in a strange environment all made Vietnam a setting where a high proneness to heroin addiction existed. In the United States, however, these same men were in very different settings, with which addiction was incompatible.

Social theorists frequently use a modified "setting" argument to suggest that the laws that have made private use of opiates illegal have themselves contributed to the spread and viciousness of heroin addiction. They say that these laws may have forced users into subcultures where excessive and compulsive use, antisocial attitudes and criminality become parts of the social learning experience and are not the effects of heroin itself. Our society's reliance on drugs—whether prescribed or sold over the counter—for easing every discomfort we experience may also indirectly endorse drug abuse. Drugs are vigorously promoted for "tension headaches" and "sleepless nights", and drug companies urge doctors to prescribe mood-altering drugs for their patients. In the 1960s and 1970s, illegal drug abuse was often supported by the popular expression "If it feels good, do it" and "Do your own thing". Many people believe that these social messages made increased drug addiction inevitable.

Psychologists have also observed that as newer ideas replace older ones—whether in the individual or in society—almost anything that suggests the past may be disregarded. Thus, when American young people were disillusioned by certain aspects of their nation's politics and practices in the 1960s and 1970s, many of them also ignored old warnings about drugs. And when teenagers begin to define their own ideas about adulthood, they may also begin to challenge the prohibitions of their parents.

Physiological Factors

The study of personality types and social influence helps classify different forms of human behaviour and relate them to each other. There are, of course, other fields of study that may yield even more fundamental facts about why people act as they do. Let us consider what neurochemistry is beginning to tell us about heroin addiction.

As described earlier, the opiates are remarkably similar to some of the body's own hormones, the group of chemicals called endorphins. The discovery of the opiate receptor sites in 1972 and of the endorphins in 1975 heralded a deeper understanding of the brain and the nervous system. Initially, scientists thought that enkaphalin, the first class of endorphins to be identified, was the only opiate-like substance in the body and that its sole job was to help block the transmission of pain when nearby cells were injured. During the next decade, receptor sites of different kinds of endorphins, including several varieties of enkaphalin, were identified. Now scientists are finding that other kinds of psychoactive (mood-altering) drugs—cocaine, Valium, and several classes of drugs prescribed by doctors to treat mental disorders—bind (attach themselves) to other kinds of receptor sites. Presumably these additional receptors exist for binding with natural non-opiate-like hormones yet to be discovered.

Even though the receptor/hormone system appears to be more complicated than was once thought, it is increasingly clear that our feelings and behaviour are somehow affected by a symphony of neurochemical messages and electrical impulses that flow along the billions of pathways of the brain. When we take drugs that affect our feelings by getting us high, we are disturbing the remarkable precision of this symphony with a tremendous overload of "false" messages.

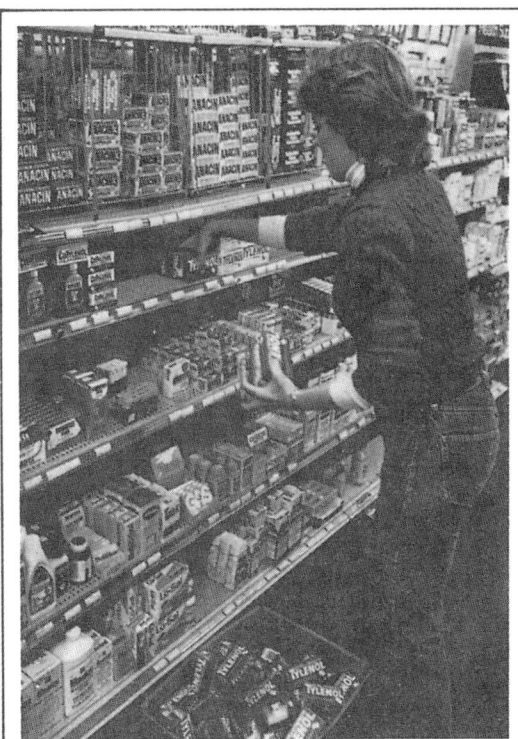

Our society relies on a wide variety of medicines to cope with everything from tension headaches to insomnia. Many sociologists believe that this unthinking "pill popping" helps to promote the abuse of dangerous illegal drugs.

An important current theory states that when a person takes heroin or morphine, the receptor sites become overwhelmed by what seems to the brain to be excess endorphins. Thus, the pituitary gland, where most endorphins are manufactured, gets a special message to halt endorphin production. Normally, the brain, which constantly monitors the body's hormone levels and needs, stops and starts the production of hormones very quickly. It does this in order to maintain exactly the right levels of the very small amounts of the many substances that keep the whole organism in balance. But when a person repeatedly floods the endorphin receptor sites with opiates, the pituitary gland shuts down endorphin production for an abnormally long time and does not easily resume normal functioning. A vicious cycle begins as the opiate user becomes more and more dependent on exogenous (externally produced) substances to cope with stress and pain.

In the 1940s researchers recognized a condition called the protracted abstinence syndrome, which addicts often experienced for weeks and months after their withdrawal symptoms seemed to be over. The symptoms of protracted abstinence—long-term avoidance of drug use—include milder discomforts than withdrawal itself, abnormal hormone levels and other signs of physiological imbalances. The syndrome may be a sign of the body's continued battle to switch on the normal functioning of the endorphin system.

There is also a theory that heroin addicts are born with faulty endorphin systems. Another theory claims that they somehow develop endorphin problems before using opiates. If either theory is true, heroin use may become an obsession because it tends to correct a bodily deficiency.

Modern science is also reviving some long-standing ideas about addiction to pleasure, the concept that heroin-induced euphoria establishes thresholds of pleasure that are so abnormally high that the heroin-user loses interest in more everyday satisfactions. This concept gained new credibility with the discovery that there seem to be receptor sites that are particularly pleasure-related. There is evidence that one group of receptors in an area of the brain called the *nucleus accumbens* is the place where endorphins and opiates bind and produce the pleasure drive of addiction. The pleasure region seems to be sensitive to many substances (including cocaine and nicotine), and it may well be that instead of wanting love, sex, good food or the satisfaction of a job well done—all of which may be expressed in subtle endorphin activity—the addict cares only for the pleasures created by the heroin.

Indeed, the brain appears to be "wired" in such a way that heroin takes the entire system literally by storm; and there is no denying the possibility that chronic heroin use changes how the brain processes feelings and experiences long after drug use ends. If that is the case, or if addicts are really suffering from a pre-existing deficiency, then perhaps finding the right kind of endorphin or substitute that could restart normal endorphin production would "cure" addiction. Researchers working on drug addiction and many other kinds of mental illness are pursuing just this line of reasoning.

Does all this mean that psychosocial concepts of addiction are meaningless? Not at all. It appears that mental states and behaviour contribute to neurochemical activity rather than merely responding to it. For example, studies suggest that endorphin levels go up in people who think they have received a painkiller but really have not. Other studies show that endorphin levels in the blood rise when people engage in certain activities that they have come to find satisfying, such as jogging and meditation. And it is quite likely that helping people change how they think about their lives, offering support and concern, and guiding them to new behaviour can affect their neurochemistry.

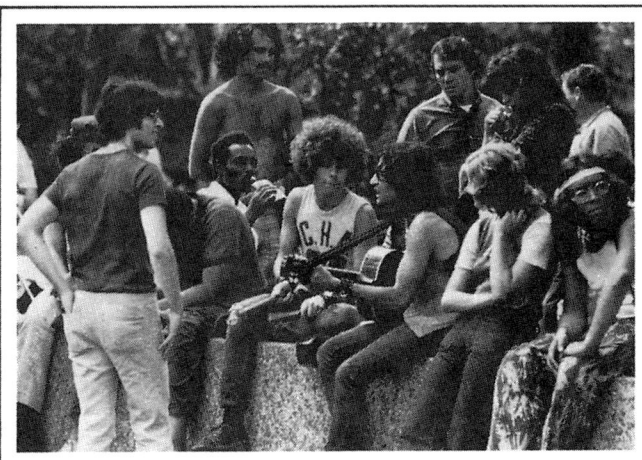

During the 1960s, teenagers began experimenting with drugs. Although heroin was not abused as extensively as drugs such as marijuana and LSD, that decade did see the introduction of this most dangerous drug into the mainstream of life.

Full recovery demands that a former heroin addict find new ways to have fun and to deal with stress. Healthy recreations such as exercise help reduce the cravings that often hinder recovery.

CHAPTER 5

THE CHALLENGE OF RECOVERY

There is no standard definition of recovery from addiction, and this makes it difficult to determine how often recovery occurs. A full recovery should probably incorporate major changes in lifestyle as well as abstinence. But, even in limiting the definition to abstinence, those who evaluate recovery face hard questions. For example, does an isolated occasion of heroin use, often called a "slip", constitute a relapse? When speaking of the length of abstinence, how does the degree of abstinence and any continuing use of other drugs affect the evaluation? One must also consider the reliability of reports of recovery. Who is doing the reporting? Treatment programmes interested in promoting their success? Former addicts who might fear acknowledging a relapse? Furthermore, heroin addiction has spread rapidly among new populations, and many new treatment services are still being developed. Therefore, the rates of recovery may be constantly changing. And finally, people who recover completely can be the most difficult people to track or identify precisely because they have so successfully shed their former lifestyles and identities.

Despite these complications, the fact that heroin addicts can and do recover is no longer in doubt. For instance, more than half the people who complete long-term residential programmes have been determined by independent researchers to be drug-free and in work years after discharge. Virtually every treatment programme that has operated for several years can point to "graduates" whose stable lifestyles are proof of real rehabilitation. If you go to any large meeting of Narcotics Anonymous, you will find many ex-addicts who have been fully abstinent for years. And the news and entertainment media often publicize the recoveries of well-known personalities who talk openly and in detail about their own success in overcoming heroin and other drug addictions. A heroin addict who truly wants to get off the drug and stay off the drug has strong grounds for optimism.

But, in one vital sense, addiction is clearly for life. Once addicted to a given class of drugs, a person retains a special vulnerability to active re-addiction should he or she ever use that drug again.

Recovery's Many Dimensions

The first step in any recovery involves the addict's decision to change. Such motivation is usually the most significant hurdle in overcoming dependency. Withdrawal is a relatively brief but trying experience, and getting through it gives many addicts justifiable pride and more resolve to take further steps.

But, because the urge to use drugs can overpower resolve, recovering addicts also need to look at how drugs have affected their lives. Earlier, we noted that doctors and researchers have cited a wide range of personality disturbances as being characteristic of heroin addicts. For instance, their personal values need deep, sustained reconsideration. Distrust of other people—especially of authority figures with whom addicts have usually come into considerable conflict—and distrust of their own basic capacity to fit in as normal individuals underlie much of the struggle to stay off drugs. For many addicts, drug abuse began in adolescence, thwarting normal personality development. For them, when recovery begins, there is considerable catching up to do. Sharing experiences with counsellors, close friends and other recovering people can be vital in this painful but restorative stage of reviewing the past. Much of the first few weeks of abstinence should be spent on this review, because it brings a person in touch with the past, points out the need for change, and helps identify problems that could lead to relapse. This period also serves to help the addict resolve feelings of guilt and to recognize the responsibilities that need to be assumed in order to build meaningful relationships.

One of the next priorities is to end relationships with active users. Even casual association with such people is risky for the recovering addict, since the incidence of relapse associated with continued contact with drug-users is extremely high. A recovering addict who lives in a neighbourhood with many users will face special difficulties. As hard as it may be to end such relationships, some of which may go back years (even childhood), it must be done.

A recovering addict therefore needs strong social support—a network of new friends who do not abuse drugs, who do not stigmatize the person as a drug addict, and who can play an active role in the person's new, drug-free lifestyle. Recovery support groups are among the best settings for making new friendships early on, and they help avoid the intense loneliness that often leads to drug craving. Moving beyond the addict and ex-addict community comes in time.

Unfortunately, sometimes family and friends of addicts prove to be a major stumbling-block on the road to recovery. In such cases they are called "enablers", because their unconscious attitudes and behaviour enable the addiction to continue. Covering up for an addict's irresponsible behaviour, failing to confront problems, and protecting the drug-user from the consequences of his or her actions are common enabling behaviours that can issue from uncon-

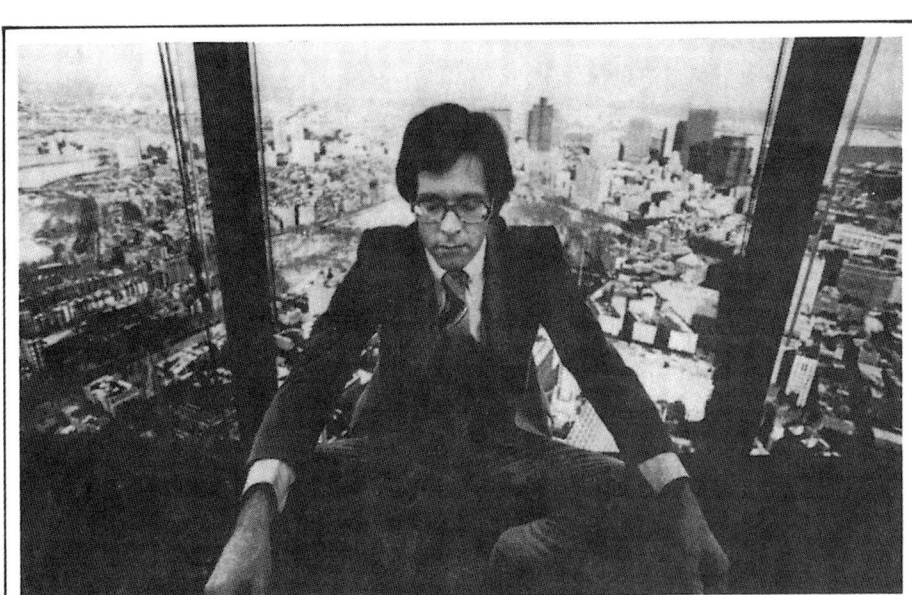

A young lawyer relaxes by peforming a yoga exercise. Unfortunately, many people in the business world turn to drugs in a misguided attempt to deal with job related stress.

scious family patterns. If another family member or loved one is an active drug abuser, all the more care must be taken to prevent an atmosphere where conflict and drug-craving can develop within the family. For these reasons, it is desirable that close relatives learn about the needs of recovery and re-examine their own family dynamics through group or individual counselling.

Not surprisingly, relationships between spouses can be the most problematic. Coming to see the past clearly often brings both partners a great deal of pain, anger and guilt. Many marriages do not survive addiction.

In addition, sexuality and sexual functioning are secret concerns of many recovering people. Opiate dependence usually impairs sexual functioning significantly, although for some addicts drugs may seem an indispensable sexual aid, at least for a while. Partners in committed relationships must share in the process of rebuilding intimacy, sometimes with the help of professional therapists.

Recovering addicts also face the challenge of finding work. Research shows that continued employment is closely related to continued abstinence; certainly the ability to stay gainfully employed is a logical sign of rehabilitation. But many ex-addicts find the authority structure, the stresses and the routine of the workplace alienating. And though they may have a need for work that nourishes self-respect and

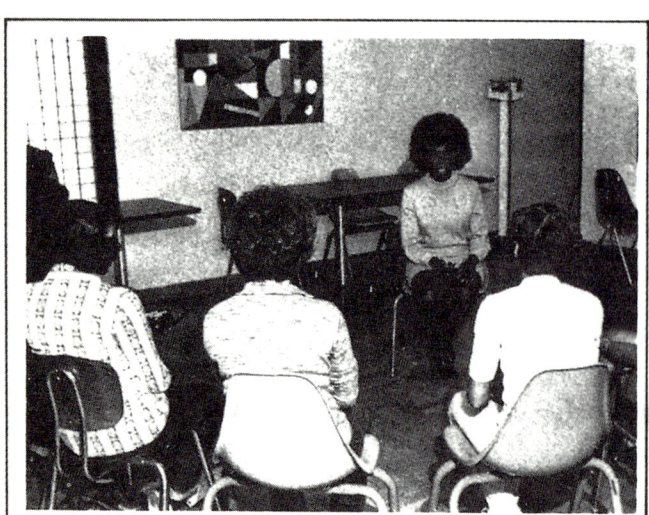

A group therapy session for recovering teenage addicts at a rehabilitation centre. This sort of counselling is particularly effective in helping young people to withstand temptation as they attempt to remain drug-free.

continued growth, few jobs offer much of either. The past can plague the job search itself. How does an untrained person find a job? And how do former addicts with poor work records, whether or not they have marketable skills, account for their past to a prospective employer? These are some of recovery's most common and puzzling problems.

Rejoining conventional society also brings with it social pressures to indulge in some other kind of drug, whether it is alcohol, cannabis or cocaine. A recovering heroin addict must learn to say no. It is one thing for a recovering alcoholic who has abused no other drugs to learn that alcohol in any amount is dangerous; but it is often more difficult for a former street addict to learn the same lesson about alcohol, cannabis and all the other drugs that always seemed mild compared to heroin. Former heroin-users often see alcohol in particular as harmless — even as the very symbol of conventionality and a good way to ease anxieties in social settings. Turning down a drink may also invite unwelcome questions about the person's reasons for doing so.

And what are the dangers of using non-opiates? Research shows that new abuse patterns are quite high among those former addicts who use other drugs. By some estimates, more than 50% develop a dependence on other drugs, even if they do not return to opiates. Abuse of alternative drugs is only part of the risk; the door to an opiate relapse often opens with the use of alcohol or other drugs. Intoxication with any substance reduces one's control, and regular use can erode resolve and judgement, allowing old behaviour to creep back. Too frequently, the desire for opiates becomes overwhelming at some point.

Dealing with physical pain is yet another danger for the recovering addict. The nervous system does not distinguish between the effects of a legitimate prescription for an opiate such as codeine, and the effects produced by an illegal dose. And laboratory studies have shown that even experienced addicts cannot easily distinguish heroin's effects from those of other strong opiates. Therefore, recovering addicts must always remember to (1) inform medical professionals about their recovery; (2) whenever possible, practise non-opiate pain therapies, such as meditation, massage, acupuncture and non-opiate medications; and (3) exercise great care when using medication, and have a supportive person monitor their drug use and reactions when painkilling medication is absolutely necessary.

De-addiction

Full recovery demands that a former heroin addict find new ways to have fun, relax, deal with stress and experience satisfaction. Here is where many recoveries fail. Too often, not enough work goes into finding new forms of recreation. Most activities that bring pleasure and satisfaction require much more effort than drug use does; they demand more practice, energy and social and skill development. So even when it comes to having fun and relaxing, recovery can mean a process of adjustment and effort.

Recreational activities that replace drug use contribute to the extremely vital process of recovery called de-addiction. The process is primarily psychological and involves the unlearning of past responses to cravings for drugs. Behavioural psychologists call such a process the "extinction" of a conditioned response.

There are established techniques for helping recovering addicts cope with this difficult process. For example, when a newly recovering addict first encounters an old friend who still uses heroin, or when tension or loneliness mounts, the person is encouraged to recall the problems that drugs have caused, become involved in other activities, and seek help from people who can provide encouragement. Many recovering addicts develop their own rituals to cope with craving drugs, such as telephoning supportive friends, reading inspirational literature, praying or meditating, and exercising. Pleasurable or stress-relieving replacement activities yield two important de-addiction benefits. First, as satisfying alternatives to drugs, they make it easier to say no to the urges to take drugs. Second, if performed regularly enough when craving develops, they can produce healthy, almost automatic responses to those things that trigger the drug-craving.

Meaningful de-addiction requires real-life situations in which the former addict has an actual opportunity to use drugs. It is widely observed that drug-craving decreases more quickly in controlled, drug-free environments such as hospitals or clinics, but the real test of self-control comes with re-entry into everyday life.

For most recovering addicts, substantial de-addiction requires at least six months to a year of gradually increasing exposure to everyday settings and events. And although former addicts may always feel some craving, with care and commitment they can reach a point at which the craving is largely a thing of the past. However, de-addiction by no means makes it safe to resume opiate use. It must be stressed that use of any opiates will put the ex-addict at risk both psychologically and physically.

Personal Reawakening

One other event seems to figure in the personal accounts of so many recoveries that it needs consideration. At a certain point during their recovery, many people experience a shift in values and perspectives. Whether they see this shift as spiritual, religious or psychological, few former addicts fail to acknowledge that recovery brings them to the deepest feelings of reaffirmation about life and its purpose. We do not know exactly how, when and why this deep inner change occurs and how it helps support other processes of growth and development. Nor can we conclude that all recoveries demand a spiritual awakening. But we must recognize that a common price of heroin addiction is the collapse of one's core—the psyche, the soul, whatever one feels it to be—and that recovery often demands no less than the transformation of a person.

Feelings of intense loneliness often precipitate drug abuse in young people. A teenager attempting to kick a drug habit usually needs to establish a network of supportive, drug-free friends.

A teacher answers questions concerning drugs. A growing number of secondary schools have established programmes to educate young people about the dangers of drug abuse.

CHAPTER 6

TREATMENT AND REHABILITATION

Our examination of heroin and heroin addiction concludes with a look at the principal forms of treatment used. This chapter starts by discussing some aspects of the legal system that provide an important background for rehabilitation and ends with suggestions about how concerned individuals can offer help to an addict or a recovering former addict.

The Law and Rehabilitation

Perhaps the most outstanding reduction of epidemic opiate addiction within large communities occurred in China after the 1949 communist takeover. The new government imposed very severe, quick sentences on drug traffickers, and addicts were subject to "rehabilitation" that involved especially hard labour and harsh political "re-education". The official punishment for relapse was execution. Many addicts who could, fled the country; many were executed. However brutal and inhuman, the policy was apparently effective. Although in recent years there have been unofficial reports of renewed opium and heroin addiction in China, most observers have agreed with official reports that claimed that addiction was virtually eliminated.

However successful the Chinese government's approach may have been in stamping out heroin trafficking and abuse in that country, such policies would of course be unthinkable in the West. In dramatic contrast to the harsh methods of the Chinese, some people in the West propose a radically different public policy: namely, legalization of the private use of heroin. They argue that if heroin use could be monitored by medical prescription or legitimate authorities, the total social cost attributed to crime and the illegal drug trade would be greatly reduced. Tax money could even go toward the treatment and prevention of drug abuse. Moreover, some advocates of legalization believe that if crime could thus be eliminated society should allow an individual to use heroin — regardless of the personal consequences — as a personal right.

Advocates of this approach often point to the practice which was once popular in Great Britain that allowed doctors to prescribe heroin for an identified group of addict patients. However, the practice of prescribing heroin to British addicts fell from favour during the 1970s; although there are still doctors and health-care services which still believe in the value of this approach, its effectiveness remains a source of controversy in Britain itself.

This Chinese poster from 1928 shows the forces of good health bludgeoning the demons of opium to death. Nowhere has the campaign against opium abuse been as intense as in China – at one time measures to stamp out drug abuse in this country included the execution of addicts.

In the meantime, the widespread abuse of heroin and related drugs continues to pose a worldwide threat to the social order. In Europe and the United States, laws attack the problem from three different directions:

1. *Supply reduction.* The idea behind this approach is simple: the less uncontrolled heroin available, the better. Not only does less heroin reduce the incidence of new addictions, but it is known that when the supply is drastically reduced within a given community, more addicts in that community seek treatment. Thus, seizing large supplies of heroin is a major priority of the government. However, in spite of growing surveillance and the assistance of many opium producing and refining nations, most experts estimate that less than 10% of the supply of refined heroin intended for illegal export is seized by the authorities.

2. *Punishment of traffickers and users.* Stiff sentencing of convicted traffickers may reduce their number and surely express society's contempt for their trade. However, the resources of top-level operators make it unusually difficult to prosecute them successfully. And imprisoning addicts—who often also operate as small-time local dealers—has not in itself been shown to lower significantly the chances of relapse. Most resume using heroin as soon as they are released. Nor are there enough prisons to hold most of these people for even short sentences; convictions for possessing heroin without intent to sell or distribute usually result in some form of legal probation. But an addict's crimes against people or property may result in other charges, and imprisonment in such cases assumes a higher priority: to protect society, at least temporarily.

3. *Court-ordered treatment.* Because lawmakers have recognized that rehabilitation usually requires steady pressure and professional assistance, many laws allow judges to order addicts to get treatment instead of going to jail. Thus, probation officers often play key roles in rehabilitation. And many treatment programmes work closely with local courts to balance legal and treatment needs.

Treatment Programmes

Drug rehabilitation embraces a wide range of professionals, styles and methods that reflect varied theories, skills and experiences. The following pages describe the major kinds of treatment programmes currently in operation in the United States and other Western countries.

Detoxification

Detoxification, commonly called "detox", aims to end physiological drug dependence. Once regarded as the essence of a successful treatment, detoxification is now generally considered only as the very important first stage of real recovery. Although one method of detoxification involves the abrupt and complete cessation of all drug-taking, this method causes intense withdrawal symptoms and involves much misery and suffering for the addict. Therefore, detoxification programmes usually make withdrawal much less uncomfortable and thus much less likely to fail because of intense drug-craving. Such programmes commonly administer to an opiate-dependent person gradually decreasing daily doses of methadone. Methadone, which is legal only on a doctor's prescription, is a powerful synthetic opiate that, when taken orally, remains active in the system for more than 24 hours without producing the intense high of heroin. It therefore allows a dependent person to function reasonably well, with no drug-craving, for more than a day after taking an appropriate dose.

Most heroin dependencies can thus be ended with minimal discomfort over the course of a 10-to 21-day weaning period; during this time, the patient must discontinue use of all opiates except for the prescribed methadone. Recent research indicates that the hypertension drug Clondine, which is not an opiate and which has few side effects, also reduces the discomfort of withdrawal from several kinds of drugs, including opiates. Other non-opiate drugs are also being developed and tested for use in easing withdrawal. Currently, however, methadone remains (by far) the drug most often used for this purpose.

Detoxification using methadone can be done without hospitalization, since opiate withdrawal is not life-threatening. But because the drug-craving often intensifies as the methadone doses are lowered, addicts are more likely to complete withdrawal if they are in a controlled environment. Most detoxification programmes try to ensure that a more complete form of treatment occurs during and beyond the detoxification stage, since detoxification alone is not an effective treatment for more than a minority of cases. That is, most people who receive only detoxification do not remain drug-free. However, the success rate for addicts being withdrawn from drugs in a residential setting can be very high with more than 75% of them achieving abstinence in some centres. The success rate for addicts withdrawing from drugs as outpatients tends to be much lower. But detoxification is only a first stage of recovery.

Methadone Maintenance

Methadone was developed in Germany during World War II as a substitute for morphine. It is a powerful dependence-producing analgesic (painkiller) whose effects are longer lasting but less intense than those of heroin. In the 1960s, the American physicians Vincent Dole and Marie Nyswander and other researchers recommended the medically prescribed administration of methadone for long-term addicts, whose bio-chemistry, the doctors claimed, required indefinite opiate doses and who could not otherwise stay abstinent. This is called methadone maintenance.

A police official in Thailand burns heroin and morphine. This is done every year; in 1981, 702 pounds of these drugs were destroyed.

In 1981, there were about 67,000 addicts on methadone maintenance in the United States. Almost all of them made daily visits to a clinic, where they took an oral dose of methadone. Clients who have demonstrated reliability were occasionally allowed "take home" doses so that they did not have to come to the clinic on weekends or during short vacations. Now, a long-acting form of methadone (L-alpha-acetyl methadol, or LAAM) that needs to be taken only three times a week is becoming more available.

Clients' urine samples are chemically tested on a regular basis to determine whether they are using illegal drugs, particularly opiates. However, moderate to high doses of methadone effectively block most opiate receptor sites from any additional opiates, so that even if a methadone client used heroin to experience a high, it would take a very strong dose to overcome the methadone block. Although oral methadone has a euphoric effect and may even, in stabilized

The director of a methadone centre talks with a patient. Good communication between the addict and a trained counsellor is essential to most drug-abuse treatment programmes. Many agencies also coordinate psychological services with vocational and educational training.

doses, somewhat reduce reflexes and mental sharpness, methadone maintenance usually allows close to normal functioning as long as other drugs are not used simultaneously. However, methadone clients often abuse other drugs, particularly alcohol, which in combination with methadone can be especially potent and dangerous.

Daily maintenance doses, which were often 100 mg or more in the late 1960s and early 1970s, are now typically 30 to 50 mg. And many clinics increasingly emphasize their counselling services and support gradual detoxification — over the course of a year in some cases — rather than maintenance. The growing number of cases of successful, continued abstinence following methadone maintenance suggests the wisdom of this policy.

As a pharmacological control over another drug dependence, methadone maintenance is controversial. Some critics note that its use is most common in poor neighbourhoods where rehabilitation of the community is really the major need. Others feel that methadone is "just another drug" that in the end provides no benefits either to society or to addicts who want to rehabilitate themselves. The original argument that for some addicts controlled dependence is the only option also remains in dispute. But for many heroin addicts methadone has allowed stability and productive functioning. There are many sides to the controversy, and whether methadone maintenance lifts addicts up or holds them down will probably remain an issue of debate in the field of rehabilitation for years to come.

Opiate Antagonists

Another drug therapy for addiction uses opiate antagonists. This therapy works somewhat differently from other drugs and is intended to counteract their effects. Opiate antagonists chemically block the opiate receptor sites within the brain but are themselves not addicting or mood-altering. They have been available to doctors for years as short-acting preparations that were used to revive opiate overdose victims. Intravenous injections of these short-acting antagonists can revive even a comatose patient in minutes, as the drug binds itself molecularly to the receptor sites in place of the opiates.

Because opiate antagonists have a greater chemical affinity

or binding power to receptors than opiates do, the longer-acting antagonists can serve a preventive purpose: protection against opiate cravings. If administered orally, the antagonist binds itself to receptors for 24 to 26 hours. Therefore, recovering addicts can take it and be rendered immune from the effects of any opiate for a day or more. The theory behind this method of treatment is that no matter what the intensity of their craving, addicts will be unlikely to use opiates since they would experience no effects from them.

Although known side-effects are minimal, opiate antagonists have been used very little since their experimental introduction in the 1970s. Acting as a temporary chemical barrier to opiates, they do nothing to remedy the psychosocial problems of recovery. Like methadone maintenance, opiate antagonists are a partial treatment at best. Their greatest value could be for recovering addicts such as medical professionals, whose work exposes them to opiates, or for other addicts who have a strong personal investment in staying opiate-free but do not trust their own impulses. However, moving from opiate antagonist therapy to "unblocked" abstinence remains for such people the greater challenge.

Psychotherapy and Counselling

At the heart of many forms of treatment is the communication between the addict and a trained counsellor. The counsellor may be a social worker, a psychologist, a psychiatrist, or an ex-addict paraprofessional. No one theory or school of thought on how to treat addiction holds pre-eminence in the field, and countless personal styles influence the way therapy is conducted. Individual therapy, group therapy and, increasingly, family therapy are all used in the treatment of addicts. And many agencies co-ordinate these psychological services with vocational and educational training.

For many addicts, counselling serves first as a sensitive confrontation with the fact of their addiction. A good counsellor—especially an ex-addict who can personally identify with the stresses of abstinence—can offer emotional support and a safe place for the expression of fears, pain and anxiety. Group therapy is also good for this process because it allows addicts to share their common experiences and evaluate them more clearly. As the addict makes progress, peer groups can be invaluable in supporting continued change and growth.

Many psychotherapists explore the psychological roots of an individual's addiction and other conditions that may have contributed to the addict's difficulties. Marital and family counselling can help identify and modify the attitudes and behaviour among loved ones that may have contributed to the onset and perpetuation of addiction.

Continued counselling following inpatient treatment can help ease the recovering addict's adjustment to life without drugs. These outpatient counselling programmes are the most common services for addicts in the United States. Because they may use any or all of the forms of therapy mentioned earlier and usually are open to addicts in any stage of recovery or addiction, as well as to users of any drug, it is extremely difficult to generalize about their value. What we do know is that the dropout rate from outpatient counselling programmes is very high; and overall, the evidence of their effectiveness is inconclusive.

Good communication between the addict and a trained counsellor is essential to most drug-abuse treatment programmes.

Therapeutic Communities

One of the most novel forms of drug rehabilitation treatment is the therapeutic community or TC. Therapeutic communities were originally proposed by psychiatrists in the late 1940s as special hospitals for psychiatric inpatients—the idea being that treatment could be enhanced if the social structure of the hospital environment itself stimulated greater self-awareness and responsibility among the patients. This kind of approach was independently adopted in the United States by the organization called Synanon, which began operation in 1958 in California as a residential community run by and for recovering heroin addicts. In part, Synanon was a rejection of psychiatric therapies, which the Synanon group saw as useless in treating addiction. Synanon relied instead upon the knowledge and insights of the addicts themselves. Typically run by former heroin-users with strong personalities, other TCs were begun during the 1960s and early 1970s; they used Synanon as their model and greatly influenced the style and philosophy of the treatment of heroin addiction.

Synanon was originally designed as a permanent residence, in the belief that outside a highly structured, drug-free, peer environment, former heroin addicts would quickly relapse. Today, hundreds of TCs provide residential therapy for thousands of clients, many of whom are chronic abusers of

Profits from "The Concept," a 1968 play consisting of improvisations by ex-addicts, went to maintain Daytop Village, a rehabilitation centre.

non-opiate drugs as well as heroin. In most cases, TCs offer 6- to 24-month programmes designed to prepare their clients both psychologically and behaviourally for life in the outside world.

TCs serve several important purposes. First, they are controlled settings in which new residents often undergo withdrawal from drugs quickly. Since most TCs endorse total abstinence from all mood-altering medications and refuse to indulge "junkie" behaviour, methadone is rarely offered. In such a setting, stopping all drug use at once can be surprisingly tolerable and uncomplicated. Many clients also enter TCs directly upon completing withdrawal at separate inpatient services. Second, many courts allow addict-defendants residential treatment instead of imprisonment, in effect putting therapeutic pressure on them to complete the programme. Third, the structure of confrontation among addict-residents appears to stimulate positive changes in attitudes and self-understanding. Most therapeutic communities also supplement their traditional self-help styles with professional counselling and therapy. The older, so-called concept TC philosophy involved tearing down the personality defences of the addict with bitter verbal abuse and humiliating punishments and then rebuilding a new self-image, using rewards for more acceptable behaviour. Today, concept TCs usually incorporate newer psychological and developmental theories in their approach. Fourth, through vocational and educational training and because the upkeep and management of many TC facilities are performed by residents, they can teach new personal and social responsibilities as preparation for discharge from the programme.

The dropout rate from TCs is high: 75% of the residents usually leave within the first six months. However, some follow-up studies have shown that as many as 90% of the clients who do complete treatment remain abstinent and in work for years afterwards. Many graduates become TC staff members themselves, and so their employment is a kind of intense and prolonged aftercare.

TC treatment is not the answer for all heroin addicts, but clearly it has been good for many people who have needed a long-term, controlled, drug-free environment and who had to overcome a serious lack of skills as well as anti-social attitudes and beliefs.

Short-term Residential Treatment

When the vast majority of heroin addicts came from poor and disadvantaged populations, publicly funded rehabilitation programmes dominated the treatment field. But as more well-to-do people have become addicted to heroin and other drugs, the number of alternative services has grown. Many private hospitals and health facilities now offer special services for both alcoholics and other drug-addicted patients who are able to pay for their services either directly or through medical insurance coverage. Typically these are 4- to 6-week programmes that provide medically supervised detoxification, education about addiction, and therapy for both patients and their families. They do not provide the personality rehabilitation or the long-term behaviour management and training of TCs, but they usually promote follow-up support (often through Alcoholics Anonymous or Narcotics Anonymous) so that patients can return quickly to job and family while still getting help in maintaining abstinence. Many of these programmes are new and compete as profit-making institutions in the marketplace. They usually retain most of their patients for the full course of residential treatment and typically report that the majority of people who complete the programme are still abstinent at 6- to 12-month checkups. Independent evaluations of their long-term success rates have yet to be made.

Self-help Fellowships

Alcoholics Anonymous (AA), which was founded in the United States in the 1930s, led the way for alcoholics to help themselves by helping fellow alcoholics. Narcotics Anonymous (NA) is a virtually identical programme. It was formed by heroin addicts who were AA members, and its groups help people who are addicted to heroin or other drugs. These two organizations hold thousands of open meetings nationwide each week, where participants can talk about common experiences and difficulties. The fellowship among participants provides powerful support, inspiration, reminders of the past and constructive role models.

The programme philosophy of the "Twelve Steps" asserts that recovery begins with an acceptance that one is powerless over intoxicating drugs. It also says that the strength needed for abstinence and personal growth does not come from will-power but rather from a "higher power"—whether it is God or some other supreme being. For most people, the Twelve Steps thus make spiritual devotion central to recovery. As with many residents of therapeutic communities, the addict may undergo a conversion experience that profoundly alters his or her values and beliefs.

Though neither AA nor NA keeps formal records on participants and so can provide no data on their success, the growing voluntary membership of these two groups in the U.S. and elsewhere suggests the important role that their meetings and philosophy can play in the recovery of the countless numbers of addicts. Many professional agencies view AA and NA programmes as valuable adjuncts to, or even central components of, the work of rehabilitation.

How You Can Help

People in our society do not grow up to be drug-free without help, they do not acknowledge and confront their own drug problems without help, and they do not rebuild lives broken by addiction without help. Here is some guidance for offering your personal assistance to people with serious drug problems.

We can help most drug-users by demonstrating that life can be lived well—even best—without drugs. This is not a moralistic cliché. Recovering addicts almost universally attest to the value of knowing people who are good role

To the addict who "shoots", the syringe is as much a part of his or her daily clutter, as the cup is to the coffee drinker or the match is to the smoker.

models. Another basic need is for helpers to learn about addictive disorders and the process of recovery and, through understanding, to respect the committed efforts an addict makes to achieve recovery.

The best cure for heroin addiction, as for any illness, is prevention. Perhaps more typically than any other drug abusers, heroin addicts come to their "drug of choice" only after prolonged use of many other substances. Therefore, in helping to combat serious problems such as teenage abuse of alcohol, cannabis or other drugs, we may be lowering the risks of future heroin addictions. And for every drug-user who gets help early and avoids heroin addiction, a community is spared enormous suffering and cost.

To help an individual who is developing a drug problem it is important to see the danger signs, since the person will rarely admit to the problem without being confronted with it. In fact, many heroin-users will admit to their use of other drugs or falsely claim a problem with other drugs (usually alcohol) rather than acknowledge that the real culprit is heroin. The visible signs of drug abuse are similar for many drugs. Typical ones are secretiveness, association with known drug-users, disturbed sleeping habits, either a washed-out or flushed appearance, glazed or bloodshot eyes, slurred speech, unusual or unaccountable expenses, frequent mood changes and deteriorating performance at work or school.

Organizations such as Al-Anon or Nar-Anon can provide both support and guidance for the friends and relatives of drug addicts.

The specific signs of opiate intoxication include abnormally constricted pupils, frequent scratching and repeated dozing off. Even more telling of a growing addiction are thefts and missing valuables, withdrawal symptoms coupled with an urgent need to leave the house (actually to get heroin), puncture marks on the skin from the injection of the drugs in the arm and, of course, the presence of drugs and the equipment needed for using them.

What do you do when these signs appear? If the presumed user is only an acquaintance, share the facts with someone who is in a position to confront that friend or loved one with your concerns, as painful as that may be. Failing to do so could eventually bring even more pain. Initially, your words may meet with denial and bitterness. At first, most users deny to others that they are using drugs, and deny to themselves that they are in trouble. But, by stating your observations plainly and without judging the person, you can show your concern and help to plant seeds of change.

If the problems continue, it is best to get additional help. Professional therapists can assist with sensitively arranged group confrontations that make clear the facts and concerns of friends, associates and loved ones, and can apply concerted pressure towards change and, in particular, towards treatment. The more troubling the user's behaviour is, the more treatment must be encouraged and demanded. Indeed, most addicts accept treatment only when the pressure to change becomes overwhelming and the support for drug use has all but collapsed. People who are close to the addict can receive support and guidance for themselves from professionals from self-help groups such as AA or NA. These organizations help people recognize and end their enabling behaviour so that the drug-user can begin to experience more of the consequences of drug use. The family of a heroin addict should become familiar with the treatment resources available both to the addict and to themselves. Finding the right way to stop enabling continued drug use takes guidance, rock-hard determination and love. It is important to remember that heroin addiction is a mortal threat and that treatment can save and restore a life. Seeking treatment must be seen as a step toward strength and health, not as an admission of failure.

Once the addict enters treatment, friends and family must

support that treatment. Ideally, those who are closest to the addict should serve as partners in the recovery, learning about the therapeutic process, and (if asked by the programme) participating in counselling sessions or other activities.

Partnership in recovery becomes even more important once the treatment is completed because the challenges of long-term recovery cannot be faced alone. No matter how committed a person is to abstinence, recovery means growth, and growth requires the guidance, encouragement and accommodation of other people. And recovery is usually a bumpy road. Like immigrants in a new culture, former addicts are often insecure and hesitate to take steps that seem perfectly simple to the rest of us. Unresolved feelings and sudden uncertainties can overwhelm, confuse and depress them. Renewed drug craving can be deeply unsettling. There may even be slips (back into drug use) that, if not confronted quickly, can lead to a full-blown relapse—a "fall"—that can destroy everything the ex-addict has built. Such difficulties demand that friends and family show both an understanding

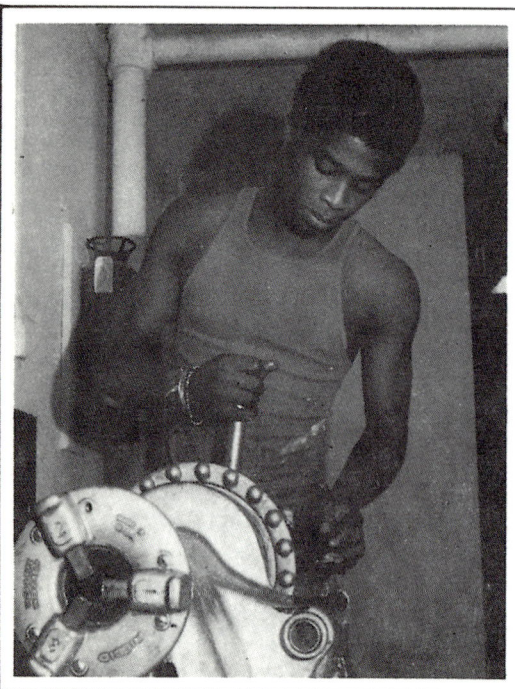

A recovering heroin addict operates a pipe-fitting machine at a rehabilitation centre. Vocational training can help build self-esteem in ex-addicts and give their lives direction.

patience and a clear expectation that the person can and will take measured steps forward. AA's famous motto says it well: "One day at a time." Long-term goals must be built slowly as a recovering person concentrates on the simple tasks of the here and now and deals with each need as it arises. With this in mind, families must stay informed and respectful of the person's plans and needs. Spouses and others must not be jealous of time spent with new friends at recovery group meetings. Old non-addict friends should encourage and welcome the person into new social activities that are non-threatening and non-stressful. And, of course, maintaining an alcohol-and drug-free environment is a priority.

Recovery from heroin addiction not only returns a person to normal life but frequently gives the ex-addict an extraordinary appreciation for the chance to love and contribute to others. To help someone recover often brings the helper a similar reward.

Recovery from heroin gives an ex-addict an extraordinary appreciation for the chance to love and contribute to others. To help someone else recover often brings the helper a similar reward.

Some Useful Addresses

In the United Kingdom:
Advisory Council on the Misuse of Drugs
c/o Home Office, Queen Anne's Gate, London SW1H 9AT.

British Association for Counselling
87a Sheep Street, Rugby, Warwicks CV21 3BX.

Department of Education and Science
Elizabeth House, York Road, London SE1 7PH.

Health Education Council
78 New Oxford Street, London WC1A 1AH.

Home Office Drugs Branch
Queen Anne's Gate, London SW1H 9AT.

Institute for the Study of Drug Dependence
1-4 Hatton Place, Hatton Garden, London EC1N 8ND.

Medical Research Council
20 Park Crescent, London W1N 4AL.

Narcotics Anonymous
PO Box 246, c/o 47 Milman Street, London SW10.

National Association of Young People's
  Counselling and Advisory Services
17-23 Albion Street, Leicester LE1 6GD.

Northern Ireland Department of Health and Social Services
Upper Newtownwards Road, Belfast BT4 3SF.

Release
1 Elgin Avenue, London W9.

Scottish Health Education Unit
21 Lansdowne Crescent, Edinburgh EH12 5EH.

Scottish Home and Health Department
St Andrews House, Edinburgh EH1 3DE.

Standing Conference on Drug Abuse
1-4 Hatton Place, Hatton Garden, London EC1N 8ND.

Teachers Advisory Council on Alcohol and Drug Education
2 Mount Street, Manchester M2 5NG.

In Australia:

Department of Health
PO Box 100, Wooden ACT, Australia 2606.

In New Zealand:

Drug Advisory Committee
Department of Health, P.O. Box 5013, Wellington.

Drug Dependence
11-23 Sturdee Street, Wellington.

Drug Dependency Clinic
393 Great North Road, Grey Lynn, Auckland.

Medical Services and Drug Control
Department of Health, P.O. Box 5013, Wellington.

National Drug Intelligence Bureau
Police Department, Private Bag, Wellington.

In South Africa:

South African National Council on Alcoholism and Drug
  Dependence (SANCA)
National Office, P.O. Box 10134, Johannesburg 2000.

A number of organizations in South Africa provide information and services in the field of drug dependence. SANCA will supply information on these, as will the government's Department of Health and Welfare.

Further Reading

Berridge, V. & Edwards, G. *Opium and the People.* London. Allen Lane. 1981.

Brecher, Edward M. and the Editors of *Consumer Reports. Licit and Illicit Drugs.* Boston: Little, Brown and Company, 1972.

Downs, Hunton. *Opium Stratagem.* New York: Bantam, 1973.

Hawkins, John A. and Grab, Gerald N., eds. *Opium Addicts & Addiction.* Salem, New York: Ayer Company, 1981.

Jaffe, J.H. "Drug addiction and drug abuse." *The Pharmacological Basis of Therapeutics,* 5th ed., L.S. Goodman and A. Gilman, eds. New York: Macmillan, 1975.

Kaplan, J. *The Hardest Drug.* Chicago. Univ. Chicago Press. 1983.

Meyer, R.E. & Mirin, S.M. *The Heroin Stimulus.* New York. Plenum. 1979.

Platt, J.J. *Heroin Addiction.* Malabar. Krieger. 1986.

Stimson, G.V. & Oppenheimer, E. *Heroin Addiction: Treatment and Control in Britain.* London. Tavistock. 1982.

Glossary

addiction   a condition caused by repeated drug use, characterized by a compulsive urge to continue using the drug, a tendency to increase the dosage, and physiological and/or psychological dependence.

addiction to pleasure   a concept that claims that heroin-induced euphoria establishes thresholds of pleasure that are so abnormally high that the heroin-user loses interest in more everyday satisfactions

adulterant   an impure, inert, weaker and/or cheaper substance, such as baking powder or quinine, that is added to a drug to dilute it, thereby often making it more dangerous to the user but more profitable to the drug dealer

alkaloid   any of various basic and bitter organic compounds found in seed plants

amphetamine   an addictive drug that stimulates the nervous system; it has been prescribed and abused as an appetite suppressant and antidepressant

analgesic   a drug that produces an insensitivity to pain without loss of consciousness

barbiturate   a drug that causes depression of the central nervous system; generally used to reduce anxiety or to induce euphoria

belladonna   a nonaddicting, powerful, mood-altering tranquilizer obtained from the nightshade plant Atropa belladonna

codeine   a sedative and pain-relieving agent found in opium and related to, but no less potent than, morphine

de-addiction   a vital process of recovery from drug use that involves the unlearning of past responses to cravings for drugs

denial   continued self-deception by a chronic drug-user about growing abuse and dependence

depressant   any drug that decreases a bodily function and/or nerve activity

detoxification   the process by which an addicted individual is gradually withdrawn from the abused drug, usually under medical supervision and sometimes in conjunction with the administration of other drugs

dysphoria   an exaggerated feeling of depression related to low self-esteem *endocarditis* a life-threatening inflammation of the lining of the heart

endorphin substances produced mainly by the pituitary gland that, in a manner similar to opiates, become attached to receptor sites on neurons, thereby helping to regulate responses to stress, pain, and many other internal and external events that affect an individual's well-being

enkaphalin a type of endorphin that helps block the transmission of pain

euphoria a mental high characterized by a sense of well-being

extinction the gradual loss of a conditioned reflex

hallucination a sensory impression that has no basis in external stimulation

hashish an extract prepared from the flowers, stalks, leaves and resin of the hemp, or marijuana, plant, which is smoked for its euphoric effects

hepatitis inflammation of the liver

heroin a semisynthetic opiate produced by a chemical modification of morphine and abused for its analgesic and euphoric effects

hypertension abnormally high blood pressure

individuation the maturation process of establishing one's own sense of identity and capacities for independent choice and actions

methadone a synthetic opiate that produces effects similar to morphine and is used to treat pain associated with terminal cancer and in the treatment of heroin addiction

morphine the principal psychoactive ingredient of opium that produces sleep or a state of stupor, and is used as the standard against which all morphine-like drugs are compared

neuron a cell specialized to conduct electrochemical signals

nucleus accumbens a region of receptors in the brain where endorphins and opiates bind and produce the pleasure drive of addiction

opiate a compound from the milky juice of the poppy plant *Papaver somniferum,* including opium, morphine, codeine and their derivatives, such as heroin

opiate antagonist a drug which, when administered, prevents an opiate from having any effect

overdose when more of a drug is taken than the amount necessary to obtain a desired effect, usually resulting in adverse effects or even death *physical dependence* an adaptation of the body to the presence of a drug such that its absence produces withdrawal symptoms

protracted-abstinence syndrome a group of symptoms that persists after withdrawal symptoms have disappeared, including abnormal hormone levels, discomfort milder than withdrawal itself, and other signs of physiological imbalances

psychoactive changing mood, behaviour, and/or thought processes

psychological dependence a condition in which the drug-user craves a drug to maintain a sense of well-being and feels discomfort when deprived of it

psychopathic a term used to describe a person who lacks the instincts that are essential for forming caring human relationships and who is resistant to the lessons of experience

receptor site a specialized centre located on a neuron that, when bound by a sufficient number of molecules, such as endorphin or opiate molecules, produces an electrical charge

sedative a drug that produces calmness, relaxation and, at high doses, sleep; includes barbiturates

septicaemia blood poisoning, or the presence of disease-causing bacteria in the blood

tincture an alcoholic extract of vegetable or animal substances

tolerance a decrease of susceptibility to the effects of a drug due to its continued administration, resulting in the user's need to increase the drug dosage to achieve the effects experienced previously

tranquillizer a drug that has calming, relaxing effects

withdrawal the physiological and psychological effects of discontinued usage of a drug

Index

abstinence, 29, 67, 92, 95–6, 113–14
  see also heroin, addiction
acquired immune deficiency syndrome
  see AIDS
adaptive theories, 84
  see also heroin, addiction
Addiction Research Centre, 37–8, 81
addictive personality, 82, 96
AIDS (acquired immune deficiency syndrome), 63–4
  see also heroin, risks
alcohol, 17, 21, 26, 34, 54, 60, 62, 71, 87, 88, 99, 109, 114, 116
alcoholics *see* alcohol; Alcoholics Anonymous
Alcoholics Anonymous (AA), 86, 114–15, 119
alcoholism, 43
  see also alcohol; Alcoholics Anonymous
alkoloid, 18
  see also opiates
amphetamines, 39, 72
analgesic, 107
  see also morphine, medical uses; opium, medical uses
aspirin, 13, 27
atropa belladonna, 29
  see also heroin, addiction
barbiturates, 39, 54
Baudelaire, Charles, 19
  see also laudanum; opium
Bayer Company, 13, 27–8
  see also heroin, synthesis
belladonna, 29
black market, 34, 36, 45, 48–52
  see also heroin, crime and; heroin, distribution and marketing
bootlegging, 34
  see also alcohol
British East India Company, 16, 21
Browning, Elizabeth Barrett, 19
Bureau of Narcotics, 33, 36
  see also heroin, crime and; heroin, efforts to control
Byron, Lord (George Gordon), 19
cannabis, 26, 39, 54, 71–2, 87, 99, 116
cigarettes, 87
clonidine, 106
  see also heroin, addiction
cocaine, 23, 26, 31, 33, 38, 54, 62, 91, 93, 99
codeine, 43, 99
  see also opiates

Coleridge, Samuel Taylor, 19
concept TC, 113
  see also heroin, addiction; therapeutic communities
conditioned response, 67, 100
conditioning, 80
Confessions of an English Opium Eater (de Quincey), 18–19
counselling, 110–14
  see also heroin, addiction
de Quincey, Thomas, 18–19
de-addiction, 100–1
  see also heroin, addiction
dependence, 64
  see also heroin, addiction; heroin, dependence; opium, dependence
detoxification, 29, 32, 34–5, 37, 106–7, 109
  see also heroin, addiction; opiates, addiction
diacetylmorphine, 27
  see also heroin
diazepam *see* Valium
disease, 78–9
  see also heroin, addiction; opiates, addiction
Dole, Vincent, 107
  see also heroin, addiction; maintenance therapy; methadone
"dope fiends", 21, 33, 36
  see also heroin, public attitudes; opiates, addiction
Dreser, Heinrich, 27–8
  see also heroin, synthesis
dysentery, 22
  see also morphine, medical uses
enablers, 97–8
  see also heroin, addiction
endocarditis, 61
  see also heroin, risks
endorphins, 61–2, 90–1
  see also heroin, central nervous system effects; heroin, mechanism of action
enkephalin, 90–1
  see also endorphins
existential factor, 85
  see also heroin, addiction
extinction, 100
  see also conditioned response; de-addiction
French Connection, 44
  see also heroin, smuggling
Galen, 14
  see also opium, history; opium, medical uses

Golden Crescent, 44–6, 56
  see also opium, production
Golden Triangle, 44, 46, 56
  see also opium, production
Gompers, Samuel, 26
  see also heroin, public attitudes
Gordon, George see Byron, Lord
group therapy, 110–11
Hague Convention of 1912, The, 30
hallucinogens, 39
Halsted, William, 36
  see also morphine, addiction
Harrison Narcotics Act of 1914, 31–3
  see also heroin, crime and; heroin, efforts to control; heroin, legal status; opiates, legal status
hepatitus, 63
heroin
  abuse potential, 13, 60
  addiction, 25
    availability, 87
    case studies, 70–5
    criminal behaviour and, 69, 71–5, 104–5, 117
    employment and, 98–9
    epidemiology, 32, 33, 41–3, 55–6, 87
    familial factors, 83–4, 88, 97–8, 111, 117–19
    personality and, 68–9, 82–6, 96, 113
    physiological factors, 90–3
    prevention, 116–19
    rehabilitation, 95–101, 115–19
    signs, 117
    social factors, 86–90, 97–8, 117–19
    stereotypes and, 22, 26, 29, 32–3, 36, 38–9, 81
    theories, 77–94
    treatment, 34–8, 71, 74, 89, 95, 103–19
  behavioural effects, 68–9, 72, 74–5, 116–18
  cardiovascular system effects, 62
  central nervous system effects, 60–2
  crime and, 32–6, 38, 48–54
  death caused by, 62–4
  dependence, 28, 64–8, 107
  distribution and marketing, 27–8, 36, 38, 48–52
  economics 41
  efforts to control, 49, 51, 54–6, 103–5
  gastrointestinal effects, 60
  history, 13–16, 24–5, 26–8, 31–9
  legal status, 32, 103–5
  legalization, 103–5
  mechanism of action, 60–2
  medical uses, 13, 14, 26
  methods of administration, 32, 62
  overdose, 62, 69, 109
  production, 41, 43–4, 46
  psychological effects, 59, 68–9
  public attitudes, 33, 38–9
  reasons for nonmedical use, 56–7
  respiratory effects, 60
  risks, 62–4
  smuggling, 45, 48–52
  synthesis, 13, 27
  use of other drugs with, 54
  withdrawal, 67–8
  see also morphine; opiates; opium
Hippocrates 14
  see also opium, history; opium, medical uses
hypodermic syringe, 18, 23
hypophoria, 83
individuation, 83
  see also heroin, addiction
John Hopkins Medical School, 36
Keats, John, 19
L–alpha–acetyl methadol (LAAM), 108
  see also methadone
laudanum, 16, 18, 19, 21, 24
  see also opium
LSD, 39
maintenance therapy, 34–5, 107–9
  see also methadone
Mao Zedong, 35
  see also opium, history
methadone, 106–9, 113
  see also heroin, addiction
methadone maintenance, 107–9
  see also maintenance therapy
milk powder, 50
  see also heroin, distribution and marketing
mithridate, 14
  see also opium, history; opium, preparations containing
Morpheus, 18
morphine, 13, 18, 49, 92, 107
  addiction, 22, 25, 72
  derivatives, 27
  discovery, 18
  medical uses, 18, 22
  see also heroin; opiates; opium; derivatives
morphinism, 25
  see also morphine, addiction
narcomania, 25
  see also morphine, addiction
Narcotics Anonymous, (NA), 86, 95, 114–15
neurons, 60–1

see also heroin, mechanism of action
nicotine, 93
Nyswander, Marie, 107
   see also heroin, addiction; maintenance therapy; methadone
opiates
   addiction, 18–19, 25, 37–8
      definition, 67
      denial, 19, 73, 117
      sexual functioning and, 69, 98
      symptoms, 25
      theories, 28–9
      treatment, 13, 28–32, 67
   antagonists, 109–10
   central nervous system effects, 60–2, 108–9
   dependence, 18–19, 25
   efforts to control, 30–8
   history, 18–19, 21–39
   legal status, 22, 30–3
   methods of administration, 15, 18
   patterns of use
      in Britain, 18–19, 23–4
      in United States, 21–5, 30–2
   physiological effects, 69
   psychological effects, 22, 69
   public attitudes, 15, 17–19, 22–6
   respiratory effects, 62
   side effects, 27–8
   tinctures, 21
   tolerance, 60
   withdrawal, 19–25, 92, 106–7
   see also heroin; morphine; opium
opium
   abuse potential, 17
   addiction, 13, 18
   central nervous system effects, 60–2
   dependence, 19
   derivatives, 13, 18
   economics, 15–21, 26
   history, 13–27
   medical uses, 14–16
   nonmedical uses, 13–14, 19, 20–2
   preparations containing, 14, 16, 21
   production, 14, 41, 43–9
   psychological effects, 15
   tolerance, 15, 18
   toxic effects, 15
   see also heroin; morphine; opiates
opium poppy *(Papaver somniferum)*
   geography, 14
   products, 13–14
   religious uses, 14
   see also heroin; morphine; opiates; opium

Opium Wars, 19–21
outpatient counselling programmes, 110–11
oxycodone, 74
Papaver somniferum see opium poppy
Paracelsus, 16
   see also opium, history
patent medicines, 25–6
   see also opium, history; opium, medical uses
Pavlov, Ivan, 67
Poe, Edgar Allan, 19
poppy *see* opium poppy
Prohibition, 33
proneness, 82
   see also heroin, addiction
protracted abstinence syndrome, 92
   see also abstinence
psychopath, 81
   see also heroin, addiction
psychotherapy, 110–11
Pure Food and Drug Act of 1906, 30
purge therapy, 29
   see also heroin, addiction
quinine, 50, 62
   see also heroin, distribution and marketing
receptor sites, 60–1, 91, 108–10
reinforcers, 80
   see also heroin, addiction
self–help fellowships, 114–15
   see also heroin, addiction
septicaemia, 62
   see also heroin, risks
Sertuerner, Frederick, 18
   see also morphine
"shooting galleries", 69
Single Convention on Narcotic Drugs, The, 54
"skin popping", 62
social learning, 88
   see also heroin, addiction
"speedball", 54
   see also cocaine; heroin, use of other drugs with
Swinburne, Algernon, 19
Synanon, 112
   see also heroin, addiction; therapeutic community
TC *see* therapeutic community
thebacium, 14
   see also opium poppy
therapeutic community (TC), 112–15
   history, 112
tolerance, 18, 64, 66
   see also heroin, addiction
tongs, Chinese, 30, 33

   see also black market; opium, history
Treaty of Nanking, 21
   see also opium, history
"Twelve Steps", 114–15
   see also Alcoholics Anonymous
"unblocked" abstinence, 110
   see also abstinence

Valium (diazepam), 91
withdrawal, 29, 64–7, 96, 113, 117
   see also heroin, withdrawal
Wright, C. R., 27
   see also heroin, synthesis
Wright, Hamilton, 30
   see also opiates, efforts to control

Fred Zackon, M.Ed., received his degree in the Human and Social Service Programme of Antioch College. He has worked with drug addicts in various clinical and research settings. Currently he is specializing in social and developmental factors involved in the recovery from chronic life disorders, and he is working to improve the effectiveness of self-help groups.

Solomon H. Snyder, M.D., is Distinguished Service Professor of Neuroscience, Pharmacology and Psychiatry at The Johns Hopkins University School of Medicine. He has served as president of the Society for Neuroscience and in 1978 received the Albert Lasker Award in Medical Research. He is the author of *Uses of Marijuana, Madness and the Brain, The Troubled Mind, Biological Aspects of Mental Disorder,* and he edited *Perspective in Neuropharmacology: A Tribute to Julius Axelrod.* Professor Snyder was a research associate with Dr Axelrod at the National Institutes of Health.

Malcolm Lader, D.Sc., Ph.D., M.D., F.R.C. Psych. is Professor of Clinical Psychopharmacology at the Institute of Psychiatry, University of London, and Honorary Consultant to the Bethlem Royal and Maudsley Hospitals. He is a member of the External Scientific Staff of the Medical Research Council. He has researched extensively into the actions of drugs used to treat psychiatric illnesses and symptoms, in particular the tranquillizers. He has written several books and over 300 scientific articles. Professor Lader is a member of several governmental advisory committees concerned with drugs.

Michael Gossop, Ph.D., is research psychologist at the Drug Dependence Unit of the Bethlem Royal and Maudsley Hospitals. He has worked extensively in the area of drug dependence, particularly on methods of treatment, and acts as a consultant on drug and alcohol problems to the World Health Organization. His work has been published in the form of more than 50 original research papers as well as in chapters, editorials and reviews. His books include *Living with Drugs, Theories of Neurosis* and *Relapse and Addictive Behaviour.*